# THE MYTHICAL QUEST

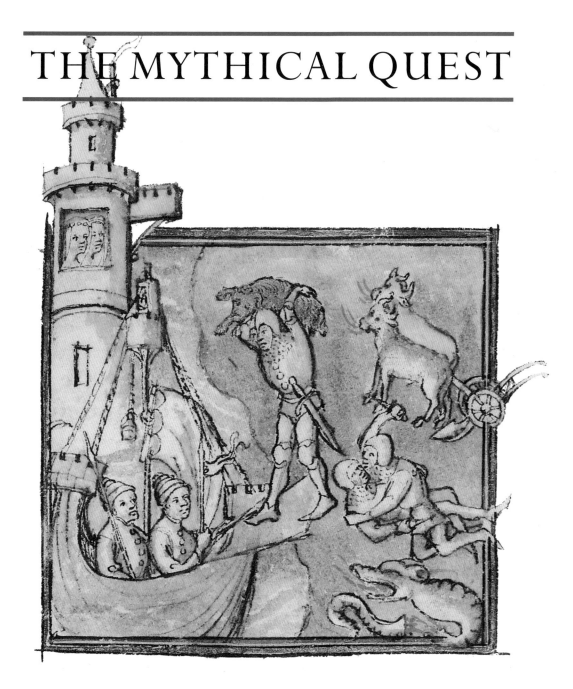

Introduction by Penelope Lively
Stories by Rosalind Kerven

WITH INTRODUCTORY TEXT AND NOTES BY
Janet Benoy Graham Hutt Jerry Losty Scot McKendrick Geoffrey West

# THE MYTHICAL QUEST

*In search of Adventure, Romance & Enlightenment*

POMEGRANATE ARTBOOKS

Half-title page: *Jason escapes with the golden fleece, behind him some of the adversaries he has overcome in achieving the quest — a pair of fire-breathing bulls, an army of warriers and a mighty dragon (see* Jason and the Quest for the Golden Fleece, *pages 8–15). Paris, c.1400.*
[British Library Add. MS 25884, f.108v]

Title-page: *The Ram-lila festival, a street theatre version of the Ramayana, showing Lakshmana about to fight with Ravana, before a large audience (see* Rama and Sita, *pages 54–63). Painting on mica, Benares, 1830–40.*
[British Library Add. Or. 4471]

THE MYTHICAL QUEST
*In search of adventure, romance & enlightenment*
accompanies an exhibition of the same title held in
The British Library Galleries, Great Russell Street, London WC1,
from June to September 1996.

The exhibition curators who contributed the chapter introductions and notes to this book were:

| | |
|---|---|
| Janet Benoy | The Seven Voyages of Sindbad the Sailor, |
| | The Tale of Cupid and Psyche |
| Graham Hutt | Journey to the West |
| Jerry Losty | Rama's Quest for Sita |
| Scot McKendrick | Jason and the Quest for the Golden Fleece, |
| | The Legendary Journeys of Alexander the Great, |
| | The Homecoming of Odysseus |
| Geoffrey West | The Quest for the Holy Grail, |
| | The Life of St Brendan, |
| | The Epic of Gilgamesh |

First published 1996 by
The British Library
Great Russell Street, London WC1B 3DG
Published in North and South America by
Pomegranate Artbooks,
PO Box 6099, Rohnert Park, California 94927

ISBN 0-7649-0008-0
Pomegranate Catalog No. A853

Designed by John Mitchell
Typeset by Bexhill Phototypesetters
Colour reproduction by York House Graphics, Hanwell
Printed in England by Clifford Press, Coventry, Warwickshire

# Contents

*Galahad, in red armour, is introduced to Arthur's court at Camelot as the long-awaited knight who will sit in the vacant Siege Perilous (from The Quest for the Holy Grail, see pages 82–90).*
[Paris, Bibliothèque Nationale MS Fr. 343, f. 3]

# Introduction

Mythology has universal resonance. Certain stories are so deeply embedded within cultural consciousness that much subsequent narrative is infused with their imageries. The characters and events of the Odyssey power a great deal of western art, both written and graphic. Without some acquaintance with this canon it is impossible to grasp the significance of much poetry and many of the exhibits in art galleries around the world. The same is true of the seminal myths of other cultures – the Ramayana and the body of narratives that we know as the Arabian Nights. These vivid and resounding fictions reflect fundamental crises of the human condition and provide the heroic figures to embody aspirations and sufferings which are universally recognised. They are of great antiquity but also of immediate relevance. They have mutated and diversified down the years as each age has seized on them and restated the themes. They have become the murmurings of a global subconscious.

The quest formula is perhaps the most central and abiding of all story structures. Quest myths include the crucial tales of both west and east – the stories of Odysseus, of Jason and the Golden Fleece, of the search for the Holy Grail, of Cupid and Psyche, of Rama and Sita. Meaning and motivation are wide-ranging in the group of myths under consideration here, but all of them include story elements with echoes elsewhere – with fairy stories, with other myths and legends and most significantly of all with one another. The narrative drive of the quest form can be seen as a metaphor for the journey through life with its attendant challenges and reversals. But within this group there is a spectrum ranging from sagas of adventure and heroic daring such as the adventures of Sindbad and Jason to such epics of spiritual endeavour as the Quest for the Holy Grail and the story of Gilgamesh. With these last, the concern is with the search for redemption and the rejection of the human condition, and craving for divine status. This is far removed from the blunt adventurism of Sindbad's narrative which seems to be a celebration of physical courage and resourcefulness, while the exploits of Jason reflect a similar spirit of heroic daring and inevitable triumph – a topic which strikes an easy accord with subsequent ages.

To examine the component elements of these stories is to be struck immediately by similarities. There are indeed contrasts in moral concern, but across the whole range of myths there runs this unifying thread – the fictional elements that crop up again and again. The setting of an impossible task, the intervention of a figure with divine or magical powers, the overcoming of apparently insuperable obstacles. The message is always one of the triumph of hope, courage and stoicism, laced with a belief that human frailty will be reinforced by divine support. There is a strong analogy with fairy stories, both in the general message of encouragement to the weak and powerless in the face of might and injustice – the classic struggle of good against evil – and such telling details as the impossible task. The trials of Psyche are strongly reminiscent of those facing the heroines of Blue Beard or of Beauty and the Beast. The stepmother who causes the expulsion of Rama and the diversion of his inheritance to his half-brother echoes the archetypal figure of fairy story and both reflect common familial situations in times of early death and many marriages. The dispossessed and persecuted child is an archetypal figure also, not only of privileged society but in every hovel. Myth and fairy story allow people to recognise their own predicament.

Oppressive tasks, malevolent relatives and undeserved misfortune are themes with an eternal relevance. Other recurring features owe less to the universal human plight than that mysterious fund of fictional images and elements which seem to enjoy a life that spans time and space. The cannibal giant encountered by Sindbad has eery similarities with the Cyclops of Homer's *Odyssey*. The seafaring adventures of both Sindbad and St Brendan include an episode in which a whale's back is mistaken for *terra firma*. Multi-headed monsters, aerial demons and benign assistants in animal form turn up again and again. Narrative problems are overcome by compacting time and endowing characters with magical powers that will allow them to dispose of distance – Hanuman the monkey simply leaps the ocean to achieve his objective, Gilgamesh walks fifty leagues in a single day. Myth invites the suspension of disbelief in that sense, but it also incorporates the primal concern with divine and magical power. It springs from the assumption that fortitude and perseverance will be rewarded with divine favour. Odysseus is supplied with a bag of winds by Aeolus. Persephone takes pity upon Psyche. And if it is not the gods who lend a hand, then the resolute will find themselves fortified by magic in the face of their difficulties.

Assumptions about divine and magical power are common to all the stories. Other notions strike a chord from one tale to another. The value accorded to marital fidelity in the Ramayana is mirrored by Homer: Sita defends her virtue at all costs, Penelope uses guile to ward off her suitors. The concept of purity pervades the search for the Holy Grail – both sexual and spiritual purity. In our own climate of thought, this can seem a curious emphasis when aligned with unquestioning acceptance of the necessity of slaughter, whether expedient or arbitrary. But the morality of myth is as uncompromising as that of fairy story – those who display courage or virtue deserve a happy ending even if they do not always get it. This is perhaps where the subtle difference lies – in fairy story all is likely to end well, mythology introduces the dark note of tragedy. The brave and the bold win through but may, like Jason, be destroyed in the process.

Universal themes, the triumph of courage and virtue over adversity and evil. Mythology has – and has always had – resonance for everyone. But the ultimate charge that it carries is that of narrative drive. The *Odyssey* is a marvellous and compelling story, furnished with unforgettable characters. The tale of Rama and Sita has elements that conjure up pictures in the mind – the dying vulture, the armies of monkeys and bears; Jason's harnessing of the wild bulls, the warriors sprung from a dragon's teeth, Medea's slaughter of her children; Psyche with the lamp in her hand, seeing Cupid. Anyone exposed to these arresting images carries them in the head forever – they become a part of a mental landscape. More than that – they open a window upon the great body of art, both written and visual, which they have inspired.

References to the *Odyssey* are built into the language itself. We talk of *an* odyssey, of being caught between Scylla and Charybdis, of seduction by the sirens' song. The pursuit of a holy grail has become a casual metaphor for some obsessive search, far removed from the spiritual connotations of the original myth. Like the language of the Bible, the imageries of myths have percolated speech – they seem to have floated free of the original sources. But they have not – they serve to tether us to a cultural heritage. That heritage is the whole subsequent effect and influence of the quest myths, the eclecticism of which is borne out in the many artistic works they have inspired. They pervade medieval manuscripts, they are a standard subject matter for heroic painting, they are a favourite choice for woodcuts and engravings. The heroes and heroines appear in tapestries, as statues, they feature on Greek vases, on miniatures and enamels. Their exploits serve up subject matter for the work of art in question, but the central figures also have the virtue of being immediately recognisable. A statue of Psyche conjures up her story.

The descent of these myths is equally diverse where literature is concerned. In the case of the written word, the myths have served as prompt and inspiration for subsequent storytellers; they have sifted down through time, woven into prose and poetry, mutating in the process. Homer's *Odyssey* surfaces in the twentieth century in such reincarnations as James Joyce's *Ulysses* and Derek Walcott's epic poem *Omeros*. On a popular level, Sindbad and other characters from the Arabian Nights are incorporated in the repertoire of pantomime. But long before that, the Greek classic myths above all provided the substance of a great raft of reference in the main body of English literature. To be without any knowledge of Greek mythology is to be mystified by thousands of references and images from Shakespeare through to Keats and Tennyson. The stories themselves are sublime; they inspire subsequent art.

We have noted the range of quest mythology from tales celebrating physical prowess to those in which the emphasis is on spiritual search. It is not too far-fetched to see echoes of these extremes in late twentieth-century fiction. The adventure story – the buccaneering derring-do of heroes such as James Bond – is a distant descendant of Sindbad. The stylised confrontations of computer games and amusement arcades seem a bizarre reflection of the recurring mythical theme of the routing of a host of enemies and accompanying mayhem. At the other end of the scale, the introspective fictions of identity crisis and the search for spiritual satisfaction would seem to owe something to the ancestral myths of spiritual quest – mind over matter.

Myths are the origin of fiction and the original language of the imagination. To read the quest stories recounted here alongside the complementary illustrations – a sample of the great range available – is to be made aware of the diversity and versatility of the myth effect. Different ages and different cultures have represented characters, events and settings according to their vision. The stories have been re-worked over time not only by poets and story-tellers but also in their countless other artistic adaptations. They are heard and seen afresh by each generation. Their antiquity is offset by their eternal appeal.

*Penelope Lively*

*The face of Humbaba, guardian of the forest.*
[British Museum Western Asiatic 116624]

# The Epic of Gilgamesh

Gilgamesh is the hero of a poem preserved on a number of clay tablets which date from the first centuries of the second millennium BC, although legends were probably circulating orally during the third millennium. The legendary hero can be traced to a historical Gilgamesh, King of Uruk in Mesopotamia (modern Iraq), who ruled *c.*2500 BC. In the *Epic of Gilgamesh* he appears as a semi-divine figure: his mother was a goddess, but he himself is clearly mortal. The tablets that preserve the poem are all written in the earliest known script, cuneiform, so called because of its wedge-shaped characters, from Latin *cuneus* meaning a wedge. However, the language of the text varies. The earliest surviving tablets are in Sumerian, but versions of the story circulated widely in Babylonian, Hittite and Elamite. The most complete version is that commissioned in Akkadian in the seventh century BC by Ashurbanipal, King of Assyria. After the latter's overthrow, the poem was lost until the mid-nineteenth century when it was rediscovered among the clay tablets dug up at Ninevah by Austen Henry Layard and Hormazd Rassam. It was subsequently deciphered by George Smith of the British Museum.

As the poem survives in fragmentary form on a number of tablets and in more than one language, the story has to be reconstructed, and gaps remain where tablets are missing. None the less, the poem clearly displays the basic form of the quest narrative. It is in two interrelated parts. The first is typical of heroic epic, telling of the winning of fame through outstanding feats of arms. Gilgamesh and his companion, Enkidu, slay Humbaba, the monstrous guardian of the forest; Gilgamesh spurns Ishtar, goddess of war, and slays the Bull of Heaven, sent by Ishtar to destroy him. The second part arises out of the death of Enkidu, who is punished by the gods for the killing of the Bull of Heaven and for other acts of *hubris*. Gilgamesh's quest is now essentially a spiritual one in spite of its physical demands, for what he now seeks is immortality. Eventually he reaches Dilmun, dwelling place of Utnapishtim, from whom he hopes to learn the secret of eternal life. Utnapishtim resembles the Jewish Noah in that he and his family survived the Deluge and preserved representatives of all living creatures. Gilgamesh successfully obtains the secret of eternal youth, but no sooner does he possess the plant of Youth Regained, than he loses it in a momentary lapse of concentration. Gilgamesh's human frailty is thus revealed and he returns to Uruk, reconciled to his essential mortality.

In addition to its basic structure, the poem shares individual features with other quest myths. Gilgamesh's physical feats transcend those of other warriors, while his spiritual search takes him on a journey beyond the known world, whence he returns without the object of his quest, but with wisdom instead. He passes through an earthly paradise (the garden of the sun god at dawn) and crosses the waters of death on his way to the land of those who have achieved immortality, the Mesopotamian Elysian Fields. He receives advice on the way: from Siduri, who tells him how to cross the ocean; from Urshanabi, the ferryman, who instructs him in how to build a boat. The story of the Deluge, which has many points in common with the Flood of Genesis, was probably not an original part of the story of Gilgamesh, but became linked to it through the figure of Utnapishtim.

WHEN the gods created Gilgamesh, they made him almost perfect. His beauty was blinding like the sun. Like a bull, his strength was insurmountable. He saw everything, knew everything. No warrior could overcome him. No virgin could resist him. People said, 'That man is like a god' – and indeed the gods had made him two-thirds divine.

But the lesser part of him, that which was human, was afflicted with human weakness. He used his allure, his strength, his power like a brute. The gods sent him to the city of Uruk and appointed him there as king; but he degraded his reign with bride-rape and bloodshed.

Suffering, the people wailed to the gods and their complaints were heard. Thus the gods created Enkidu the wild-man to be Gilgamesh's companion, to rein him in and be his soul-mate. They made Enkidu rough and unkempt; but his soul and his heart were pure. They put him to graze like a vagrant beast in the wilderness; and then they sent a woman, a harlot, to make him tame. For seven days and nights he lay and lusted with this woman, and when that time was over, he was transformed, civilised, a man. Then the woman led him to Gilgamesh.

Enkidu tamed Gilgamesh as the harlot had once tamed him. The beautiful one and the savage one: the gods fitted their destinies together like dark and light. They wrestled together, they shared visions and shadows from their souls. They learned to love each other like brothers. Each one controlled the other's brutish urges, and now the people of Uruk could pass their days in peace.

But for the demi-god Gilgamesh, such peace was not enough. He was like a bull incarcerated, and longed to stride across the world, longed to test himself. So he said to Enkidu his soul-mate, 'I am going on a journey to the Land of Cedars. I shall penetrate the forest and destroy the evil that lurks within. Come with me, my brother.'

Enkidu said, 'Your proposal strikes chill into my heart, for the Land of Cedars is guarded by the monster Humbaba, who is armed with seven-fold terrors. But because I am your brother, your will shall override my own.'

They sought blessings from Shamash the Sun god, for the Land of Cedars was his. Then they began to walk. They walked fifty leagues in a single day, they crossed seven mountain ranges. They went through the gate into the forest, in to the Land of Cedars. They made offerings to the gods, they dreamed strange dreams.

They found Humbaba the monster, the one who breathed fire, the one who charged like a battering ram. Gilgamesh withstood him. He took his axe and, with mighty blows, he felled the seven cedars. One by one he felled them; Humbaba shuddered and shrivelled. Lifeless and broken, the cedars lay there, chained at the foot of the mountain.

Humbaba too was broken, the guardian of the forest. Now weak and humble, he begged for mercy. But Enkidu, in this wild place, was wild again, and urged Gilgamesh to complete his hero's task. Together they struck Humbaba with three mighty death blows. The forest was shaken. Chaos shuddered across the world. Even the gods trembled.

And Gilgamesh gloried in himself.

*Gilgamesh and Enkidu slay the Bull of Heaven.*
[British Museum Western Asiatic 89435]

\* \* \*

Afterwards, Gilgamesh dreamed. Enkidu listened to these dreams and wove into them the thread of meaning. He saw from them that Gilgamesh was destined to be supreme, but not immortal. Yet the soul of Gilgamesh was scarred by the arrogance of fame. Dressed in king's robes, he let his virile beauty dazzle all who beheld him: the people of Uruk and even the gods in the firmament.

Ishtar, the goddess of love, offered herself as his bride, but he spurned her. She went to her father Anu – father of all the gods – and pressed her complaint, urging that Gilgamesh's arrogance should bring about his destruction.

Anu listened. He gave Ishtar the Bull of Heaven. She loosed it in Uruk and set it to destroy the people and the city. But Enkidu leapt on the bull and seized its horns. Then Gilgamesh slit its throat and cut out its heart. He plated the bull's horns with lapis lazuli and hung them on his palace walls, then paraded in victory around the city; for he, Gilgamesh, the hero-king, had overcome the revenge of the gods.

But the victory was hollow. For afterwards Enkidu dreamed of his own death and wept.

Gilgamesh, hearing his brother weeping, looked beyond victory and saw that the end of all life is sorrow. Then Enkidu sickened and died, shamefully in his bed like a woman. His shame, his departure from his brother's side, these were the gods' punishments, their vengeance for the death of Humbaba and the Bull of Heaven. Gilgamesh was broken by the weight of such a punishment. He mourned, he writhed and suffered. He wandered into the wilderness, drinking only bitterness, feeding only on despair.

\* \* \*

In time he grew satiated with grief, and set out on a new journey. His quest was to find King Utnapishtim, the one to whom of all mortals, the gods had granted the gift of everlasting life. Gilgamesh thought that if he too could obtain such a gift, he could overcome his despair.

He walked many leagues. He passed fearlessly through wild and desolate places. At length he came to the Mashu Mountains, whose gate was guarded by the Man-Scorpion. That is the gate which is always closed, the dark gate through which no human may ever pass.

Gilgamesh cried 'Open the way that is barred to me!' And the Man-Scorpion yielded, and let the hero through.

Gilgamesh walked into the darkness. It was thick like a blanket, suffocating. He walked on and emerged from the darkness into sunlight. Now he was in a garden whose bushes bloomed with gemstones, the Garden of the Gods.

Shamash the Sun God saw him and urged him to turn back. 'You will never obtain what you have come for, Gilgamesh. You, the god-like one who is also human – Everlasting Life has not been granted to you.'

But Gilgamesh answered: 'I have come this far. I cannot give up until I reach my journey's end.' So he walked on, through the softness of that Garden.

He came to the place where Siduri sat, fermenting wine to nourish the gods. She watched him coming, saw how his perfection was tarnished by despair. He poured out to her his sorrow, his fear of death, his grief for Enkidu. Siduri was not moved by him. She said, 'Gilgamesh, you are partly human, and the end of your road must be death.' Then she pointed him to the path that runs across the Ocean. 'If you wish to travel further you must seek the help of Urshanabi the ferryman.'

Gilgamesh walked to the shore of the Ocean, where he met Urshanabi and again told his story. He showed Urshanabi the despair that, like a worm, was gnawing away at his soul.

Urshanabi said, 'I have already seen this despair of yours, as you walked towards me. I saw how it inflamed your arm to cut down the forest as you passed. Because of this I am powerless to help you, for you have also destroyed my boat.'

Gilgamesh was shamed. He reined in his emotions, he fetched wood, he built the ferryman a new vessel. Then they sailed across the Ocean for many days. Gilgamesh forsook pride. He himself thrust the boat across the waters of death. He stripped himself, held up his arms for a mast and his covering for a sail. At last they arrived at the place of the sun's transit, east of the Mountain.

In this land, Gilgamesh came at last to the Faraway King, Utnapishtim, the one upon whom the gods had bestowed everlasting life. Gilgamesh paid homage to him. He told his story of glory and grief, and how his heart was ravaged by despair. Finally, he said, 'Wise father, reveal to me this mystery; how may I enjoy everlasting life?'

Utnapishtim listened and then spoke. He said, 'I did not crave immortality for myself. The gods granted me this gift because I alone saved humankind and all creation from the flood. But Gilgamesh, your supplications, your searching, your longing – all this will achieve nothing, for your divine perfection is tainted with human blood, and you must know that humankind can have no permanence.'

But Gilgamesh the hero, who had dragged himself through the depths of suffering, who had passed through the dark regions and the golden places of the gods, who had sailed beyond the waters of death – still, he would not submit. He replied, 'One-third of my being is only human; yet the remainder is of the gods.'

Utnapishtim answered, 'Maybe this is the truth; I will test you.' He challenged Gilgamesh to deny sleep for seven days and seven nights, in the fashion of the gods. And Gilgamesh failed.

Now the hero was defeated. He bathed and dressed in new clothes, then turned away and prepared to return on the long journey to Uruk. As Utnapishtim saw him go he said, 'Gilgamesh, I have a wife. With her woman's heart she sorrows at your suffering. She speaks of a magic plant which grows beneath the Ocean, the plant that mortals call the 'Mystery of the Gods'. He who eats it will find his youth restored to him again. Search for it Gilgamesh; and if you find it, seize it, guard it, keep it. Then your long journey through the wilderness will not have been in vain.'

Now Gilgamesh was comforted. Softened by humiliation, he said, 'If I find this plant, I shall take it back to Uruk and share it with my people. I shall give it to the old men to eat.'

Then he sailed again across the Ocean with the ferryman, and his hero's strength returned to him. He dived beneath the swirling waters and seized the magic plant. Overcoming its searing prickles, he freed it from the Ocean bed; the waters, in homage to this feat, carried him safely along to the home shore.

With this plant he now possessed the promise of eternal youth. Like precious stones he carried it with him, his gift for the people, a kingly gift, a hero's gift. He walked. Night fell and he stopped to rest by a well of cool water. He stripped off his king's robe and bathed.

His journey's end was close. But in the well there dwelt a serpent. The serpent smelled the plant; it smelled the scent of eternal youth and longed for it. Gilgamesh, bathing, renewing himself, relaxed his vigilance. The serpent crept forward and snatched the plant away.

It was gone. Gone in a serpent's clutch, sunk beneath the deep cool earth waters, heroically won, easily lost. And Gilgamesh wept.

Thus he returned to Uruk. They carved his story in stone, that his deeds at least might live forever. Proud were the people to have him as their king. Yet in his own heart, he was ever a servant of despair.

# Jason and the Quest for the Golden Fleece

As early as the composition of the *Odyssey* (*see* pages 16–23), the story of Jason and his quest seems to have been well known. Not only does Odysseus follow in the steps of someone whom the ancient Greeks thought of as having lived at a time before the Trojan War, but, as the hero is told, the story of Jason was already on everyone's lips. Its origins are therefore in the oral tradition out of which Homer's *Iliad* and *Odyssey* grew.

Yet, unlike Odysseus, Achilles, Hector and the other heroes of the Trojan War, Jason has not survived in any such early epic poem. Instead we have only passing references to him by such early authors as the poet Hesiod, and have to wait until 462 BC before a full, if at times allusive, account of Jason's quest was undertaken. At this point the Boeotian poet Pindar retold the story in celebration of the victory at the Pythian games of Arkesilas, King of Kyrene, who claimed descent from one of Jason's companions on the *Argo*.

Subsequently, although Jason appeared on the Greek stage in such tragedies as the *Medea* of Euripides, it was not until the Hellenistic period that he became the subject of a full epic account of his quest for the Golden Fleece. Together with the dependent Orphic *Tale of the Argonauts*, or *Argonautica*, the *Argonautica* by the third-century scholar-poet Apollonius of Rhodes established the main story-line for succeeding generations of readers.

During the medieval period the story of Jason continued to be read in two main contexts. The first was as part of Ovid's *Metamorphoses*, the popularity of which was revived in the twelfth century and further promoted in the first half of the fourteenth century by the creation of two moralised versions of the classical text. Offshoots of this important moral tradition, according to which the worth of such pagan stories lay in the further support they offered to the doctrines of the Christian Church, included the *Epitre d'Othea* by the early fifteenth-century Parisian author Christine de Pisan. The second context was entirely different, namely as part of the entertainment offered by the romance tradition. Based on the spurious eye-witness account by Dares of the Trojan War, the medieval Romance of Troy offers some justification for the abduction of Helen by Paris in telling of the first destruction of Troy at the hands of Jason, Hercules and the other Argonauts, as they made their way towards Colchis. At the head of this rich literary tradition lies the huge twelfth-century poem by Benoit de Sainte Maure, the *Roman de Troie*. Of particular importance for the preservation and continuing popularity of Benoit's text was a Latin prose version composed around 1270–1287 by the Sicilian judge, Guido delle Colonne.

Inspired by such texts as those of Benoît and Guido, one of the most powerful rulers in western Europe, Philip the Good, Duke of Burgundy, instituted in 1430 the famous chivalric Order of the Golden Fleece. Jason's patronage of this order was, however, dogged from an early date by such critics as Jean Germain, who brought into the limelight the less attractive and morally suspect aspects of Jason's character and deeds. Was it really right and proper for one of the most select groups of nobles to be seen to have as their model a man who had acted so deceitfully? Consequently the Order sought a new patron in the impeccable Biblical figure of Gideon.

By the sixteenth century such moral criticisms appear to have receded. Like such other heroes as his

*Jason rows out from Colchis (watched by Medea and other women) to the island where the ram is kept. He yokes the pair of fire-breathing bulls, ploughs the field and sows the dragon's teeth; he then cuts down with his sword the dragon which guards the golden ram.*
[British Library Royal MS 20 D.i, f.33v]

companion Hercules, Jason became a fine example of heroic achievement, his complete triumph over the many tasks set him and attainment of the supreme goal a model for all who aspired to personal gain. The Fleece now became the pot of gold at the end of the rainbow, the quest for which was celebrated openly following the voyage of Columbus and the discovery by the West of the riches of the Americas and the East Indies.

By the eighteenth century, although still a frequent subject of literature, music and the visual arts, Jason's more shabby aspect became the focus of attention. With a cynicism characteristic of the age, writers and painters portrayed Jason's attainment of the Fleece as a telling image of the exploitation of trust and romantic love. Jason's achievements were possible only because Medea was so in love with the hero that she was willing to do anything she could to help him. After she had served her beloved hero's needs, her reward was desertion. So potent an image did the story offer of love sacrificed to material gain.

Nearer our own times Jason and his quest have become again either an inspiring model or just a plain exciting story. Frequently the audience is our children, sometimes the child that remains in us. Like images of Raleigh as a boy looking out across the sea, Victorian retellings and images of the young Jason seeking glory, such as that in Charles Kingsley's *Heroes*, were meant to inspire British children on to great deeds on behalf of the Empire. More recent American reinterpretations, including some Hollywood blockbusters, have emphasised the exhilaration of Jason's heroic fight against the fantastic and evil terrors that seek to stand between him and his splendid goal. As for so many previous generations, his story continues today to offer new opportunities for both storytellers and moralists.

THE man who passed through the city gates of Iolcos and hurried straight to the royal palace was tall and sun-bronzed, arrogant and muscular, with the easy swagger of youth. When the guards challenged him, he shouldered them aside, demanding to be led to King Pelias.

The king had heard him coming, and was preparing to punish this intruder with his own sword. But his resolve failed as the young man entered the throne-room; for he was wearing only a single sandal, and Pelias had long shuddered under an oracle's warning that disaster would follow in the footsteps of a man who was only half-shod.

The youth did not hesitate in hope of a welcome. Instead, he cried,

'Listen, Pelias! I am Jason, your nephew. Your brother, Aeson, is my father, whom you deposed and threw into a miserable exile. You did not even know of my existence, did you? My father had me smuggled to safety in the wilderness, and commissioned Chiron the centaur to raise me there, schooling me in the skills of a prince. Now I am come of age and my education is complete, I intend to avenge my father and claim back his throne.'

King Pelias regarded Jason through narrowed eyes. He did not relish the prospect of another brute battle for the kingship, but he saw how Jason burnt with a ripe youth's desire to prove his might. For some time he made no reply as he searched through the devious passages of his mind for an escape. At last he spoke:

'Listen Jason, I have something equally intriguing to tell you. You may have heard that, long ago, Poseidon created a winged ram with a golden fleece and sent it to rescue Prince Phrixus and Princess Helle of Thebes from the murderous intentions of their stepmother, Queen Ino. Unfortunately, both those innocents met a tragic end: Helle fell from the ram's back as it flew with them across the sea; whilst Phrixus reached safety and married, only to be murdered by his own father-in-law. Their tragedy is compounded for us both, Jason, since those young people were our distant kin. The murderer I mentioned is called Aeëtes: he is king of Colchis, and the fleece of that golden ram is still in his possession, hidden in his realm in the sacred grove of Ares, guarded ceaselessly by a malevolent dragon.'

'Jason, I will strike a simple bargain with you. Sail to Colchis, avenge the death of our cousin, seize the fleece and bring it back here to me. In return, I swear I shall grant your request and relinquish the throne.'

Jason responded with scornful laughter. He seized Pelias' sword, flung it to one side, and shook hands with his estranged uncle to seal the improbable deal. Then he burst out from the palace and ran through the city streets, all the while shouting out details of his mission. As the news spread, scores of other young adventurers came out to meet him, jostling to join in the quest. Amongst them were many already famed as heroes: Hercules and Theseus, Nestor and Orpheus . . . and behind them came Argus the craftsman, who vowed he could fashion for Jason

*Pelias persuades Jason to build the Argo and depart on his formidable quest to bring back the Golden Fleece from Colchis.*

the most splendid ship in history, to bear him and his companions to Colchis.

That ship, the *Argo*, was swiftly built. It had fifty great oars and a figurehead carved from a sacred oak, blessed with the gift of prophesy. Jason urged his followers to waste no time, naming them the 'Argonauts' and calling them at once to set sail. Each man was eager to prove his tenacity and fortitude, so they followed a route of fortune, chosen by the winds. It led them first to the land of Lemnos, inhabited solely by hospitable women; but they tasted its pleasures only briefly before firm resolve sent them on their way. Next they were blown to an island where the elderly monarch, Phineus, was being persecuted by evil harpies; they allowed themselves an interlude just long enough to rescue him. On they went, navigating many horrors such as the clashing rocks of Symplegades; but no hazard or distraction was ever enough to delay them.

*Jason fighting the dragon which guards the golden ram. The boat in which he reached the island awaits his return. The pair of fire-breathing bulls are yoked in the background.*

[British Library Add. MS 10290, f.106v]

In good time, they came to Colchis, where a throng gathered to watch as they dropped the *Argo*'s anchor. Then Jason leaped ashore and hastened to King Aeëtes' palace, making his entry in his customarily flamboyant and impatient manner.

'If you have come here for some specific purpose, young man,' said Aeëtes acidly, 'it would be in your interests to state it before I have you arrested.'

Jason was frank in relating the details of his quest. Like Pelias, King Aeëtes perceived that this brawny youth would not easily accept a blunt refusal; he too decided to defer his reply with a challenge. So he said,

'You must realise, Jason, that this uniquely precious Fleece cannot simply be yours for the asking. If any man wishes to win it from me, he must first successfully complete a set of tasks which, by common assent, are deemed to be virtually impossible.'

Jason listened, taut with anticipation.

'First,' said King Aeëtes, 'you must go to a field behind my palace, where I keep two fierce wild bulls. These bulls have hooves and horns of polished sword-bronze, and their breath is pure flame. Tame them for me.'

'Second, you must harness these bulls to a plough, made of hard, blunt stone. Use this to plough up a weed-infested stretch of land that has never before been cultivated.'

'Next, you must sow this newly ploughed field with the teeth of a dragon. They will spring up immediately into a mass of dangerous, armed men. Kill them all.'

'Finally, you may go to the oak tree in Ares' grove, where the Golden Fleece hangs. There you will see a huge and venomous dragon tightly coiled around the tree trunk, watching day and night for enemies and thieves. Slay the dragon, Jason. If you can do that – then certainly, I will let you have the Golden Fleece.'

Without hesitation, Jason accepted the daunting challenge. King Aeëtes chuckled to himself at such callowness as Jason hurried out of the palace. But he had not reckoned with the pernicious schemings of his own daughter, Medea.

This young woman's heart was as dark as her shadow: she was a sorceress of considerable skill. Despite her breeding and her wealth, no suitors had ever been attracted to her unorthodox charms. She had been in the throne room when Jason burst in: she had watched him, listened, and been suddenly stirred by desire. She could see, it would be a simple matter to ensnare him.

*Jason escapes with the golden ram.*
[British Library Stowe MS 54, f.38v]

So she followed him out and restrained him with soft words and a light hand upon his shoulder. Jason turned to her, and found himself held by the black stars of her eyes.

'Listen,' she whispered, 'the tasks my father has set you are truly impossible – even for one as fearless and invincible as you.'

Jason did not deny it.

'But for me – nothing is impossible,' said Medea. 'I can complement your own already formidable powers, Jason, for I have trained in the ancient secrets of magic. I can weave spells to make you indestructible and give you super-human strength: I can help you.'

He swayed like a man intoxicated, and answered, 'If I fail in this quest, I am sure the shame would kill me. You give me no choice: I must accept your help, princess. What payment do you require?'

'No payment,' said Medea, smiling slowly. 'Only you. For my husband.'

Jason had little time to think, and he was in no position to bargain. Blinding himself to thought of the future, he nodded his assent.

*Medea appears in a magic chariot pulled by fire-breathing dragons in which she has escaped imprisonment, and throws the dismembered bodies of her two children in front of a horrified Jason and his companions at a banquet.* [British Library Royal MS 20 D.i, f.37v]

Then Medea led him into dark, private chambers. Here she annointed him with magic potions, and chanted obscure spells. Then she took him into the temple of Hecate, triple goddess of magic, ghosts and witchcraft: in the cold gloom, she bound him to an oath that, if ever he took home the Golden Fleece, he would also take her to be his wife.

The next day dawned. Jason strode out, wearing no armour but his own assurance, drawing on the hidden well-spring of Medea's gifted power. A great crowd was gathered there to watch him.

Then he achieved the impossible. He tamed the fire-breathing, bronze-horned bulls; he cultivated the barren field with a blunt stone plough; he sowed it with dragon's teeth. When the teeth sprang up into a menacing army, he threw a rock into its midst and laughed as the soldiers turned on each other and quickly destroyed themselves.

Now his quest was near fulfillment. Success surged through him, gave him the energy of a god. Fearlessly, he ran to Ares' grove, threw Medea's sleep-herbs into the dragon's eyes, slaughtered it, and climbed the oak tree. Then he seized the Golden Fleece!

King Aeëtes, watching in disbelief and regretting the rashness of his offer, flew into a rage. He screamed at his guards to arrest Jason and retrieve the Fleece for himself. But Medea's response was even swifter. Wearing the new status of his betrothed wife, she impelled Jason to flee, launch the *Argo* without delay and row at once from Colchis.

As the wind caught the vessel's sails, Jason became aware that Medea was not travelling alone, for beside her stood Apsyrtus, her young child brother. Medea, glancing back at the disappearing shores of Colchis, nodded coldly at the child and murmured, 'Soon this wretch will prove to be useful.'

They had not been sailing for long before a war-ship was spied behind them in hot pursuit, with King Aeëtes at the helm. As if on a signal, Medea pushed Jason aside. Then, before the whole crew's eyes, she snatched up the child, cut his throat, chopped his body into pieces and hurled them into the sea.

'This is to delay my father,' she hissed. 'He is bound to stop to gather up the remains of his little boy and honour him with a proper burial. While he dithers over his grieving, we can take our chance to get away.'

Aeëtes halted his pursuit as she had predicted: numbed with horror at their saviour, the Argonauts escaped. But now Jason's youthful fervour was all erased, and a deep chill penetrated his heart. Stained with complicity in callous child murder, he began to see the Fleece no longer as a noble prize, but as an ill-omened burden.

Thus subdued, the Argonauts sailed on. They passed safely through the perilous rocks of Scylla and Charybdis. They withstood the deathly sweet songs of the sirens. They escaped a boulder-hurling giant. All the while the Golden Fleece hung from the ship's mast; but its brilliance could no longer blind Jason to the heavy price he had paid for it.

They arrived back at Iolcus. King Pelias was astonished and appalled when Jason presented him with the Golden Fleece; but fear of the gods compelled him to honour his promise and step down from the throne.

Jason's father Aeson, was brought back from exile and crowned once more as the rightful king. But he had faded away into a bitter, decrepit old man, with his mind wandering. Medea, unbidden, bewitched Aeson and worked a miracle. She fed him with powerful herbs and performed weird rituals; she cut his throat, drained out his blood and refilled his veins with a potion that restored and renewed both his vigour and his mind.

After that, many people came in search of her macabre cures. Amongst them was the old usurper, Pelias. Medea, disdainful of the consequences, left him in agony to die.

Then the people rose up and drove Medea from the city. Jason was forced to go with her and for ten years they were exiled together in Corinth. Then Jason retrieved enough courage to abandon her, and took a young princess, Creusa, as his new wife.

The spurned Medea sent them evil wedding presents: a poisoned robe, and a palace fire that burnt her rival to death. Then she summoned Jason and murdered their own two children in cold blood before his eyes. Finally she flew from her crimes in a chariot drawn by two dragons, and was never seen again.

Jason, briefly and gloriously a hero, was now a totally broken man. He lurked by the seashore, haunting the rotting hulk of his brave ship the *Argo*. There he died before his time, crushed by its ruin and his own shame.

# The Homecoming of Odysseus

The epic Greek verses that form what we now know as the *Odyssey* and have been attributed since classical antiquity to the blind poet Homer stand at the head of a long tradition of literary and artistic reference to the story of the Greek hero Odysseus. Wherever it has been known to writers and artists, Homer's account of Odysseus's ten-year long homecoming from the Trojan War has been particularly influential. Some explanation for such interest lies in the central figure, as presented in the *Odyssey*. For Homer's Odysseus is a latent character, human, credible, but capable of being regarded in many ways. His outstanding attribute is his mind: although, like many other heroes, he has great physical strength, it is ultimately his mental resources that carry him through to the end of his quest. Such abilities can of course be equally perceived as what enables us to rise above our environment or merely to trick it.

For Aeneas, his fellow Trojans and later, the Romans, who, following Vergil's claims in the *Aeneid* saw themselves as descended from the victims of the Trojan Horse, Odysseus was the arch-deceiver and villain. Before the recovery of Homer's text by the Latin West in 1354, the Romance of Troy, as initiated by Benoit de Sainte Maure towards the end of the twelfth century, also reflected the bias of its principal source, the purported eye-witness account of the war by the Trojan Dares. In this medieval literary tradition Odysseus was the most devious of men. His story was mainly told as one of the Greek leaders who brought about the fall of Troy and on their return home suffered horrible deaths; very little is said about (and very few illuminated miniatures depict) his return voyage.

In contrast Renaissance writers and artists brought Odysseus forward as an example of the resourceful individual, whose intelligence and physical strength enabled him to overcome all the obstacles put in his way. His resistance to the seductive charms of other women leads on to his reunion with his wife Penelope, and his survival of the chaotic forces of the wider world to his restoration of order in his own kingdom. From this time onwards Homer's account of the homecoming of Odysseus gained further readers through numerous translations into the main western European languages and inspired extensive narrative cycles in wall paintings, tapestries and printed book illustrations.

By the seventeenth century less sympathetic and openly hostile views of Odysseus had returned. Preference for the Latin literary tradition and a stricter code of courtly manners combined to cause the French author René Rapin, for example, to portray the hero as an uncouth villain who repeatedly used deceit to further entirely selfish aims. Thus by the early eighteenth century when he wrote his translation of the *Odyssey*, Alexander Pope had much to do to restore the reputation of his central character. Although Pope's translation was extremely popular during the eighteenth century, English romantic poets were drawn to Homer through the earlier translation of George Chapman. Charles Lamb and John Keats, for example, found more to their taste in Chapman's fervour and mystical charm.

In our own century several reinterpretations of the story of Odysseus have been written. Two of the most important of these, *Ulysses* by James Joyce (first published 1922) and *The Odyssey: A Modern Sequel* by Nikos Kazantzakis (first published 1938), underline the rich fertility of Homer's account in their broadly opposite points of view of Odysseus. Joyce concentrates on the forces pulling back his Odysseus, Leopold Blum, to 7 Eccles Street, Dublin, whereas Kazantzakis explores the consequences of his hero's restless, questing spirit, unable to settle upon his return home and soon engaged on yet more adventures.

*The fall of Troy. The Trojan horse, the Greeks' famous stratagem by which they deceived the Trojans and finally gained entry to the city, is wheeled through the city walls.*
[British Library Stowe MS 54, f.203]

THE island realm of Ithaca was without a king. Laertes, the old monarch, had grown too frail of mind and body to rule, and his grandson Telemachus was a diffident and inexperienced youth. By right the throne should have been occupied by Odysseus, a man of whom everyone spoke with great respect, but twenty years before he had sailed away to join the war against Troy and had never returned.

His queen Penelope had courage and patience enough to wait for him. Many men of good breeding came to her palace, reminding her that Odysseus was most likely dead and urging her to choose a new husband from amongst them. But, unwilling to share either the kingdom or her bed with a stranger whose heart she could not totally trust, Penelope always declined.

As time passed the marriage proposals grew more pressing and less courteous. Now the nobler suitors had become disillusioned by her unwavering refusals; so others came to seek her hand, whose main qualities were crass, brute strength. They infiltrated the palace grounds, a rough and quarrelsome band of rivals who could not be persuaded to leave. Finally Penelope grew afraid, and realised that she would have to choose one of them soon, or risk the choice being made for her by violent means.

So she addressed the assembled suitors.

'My lords, you will be pleased to hear that soon I shall decide upon a new husband. But to be sure that the man I choose is fit to be king, I propose to set a simple test. I have a wonderful bow which many years ago belonged to my first husband, Odysseus. I will ask each of you in turn to string this bow and to use it to shoot an arrow through a straight line of twelve bronze axe-heads. I must warn you that this task is more difficult than you might expect. The first man who successfully completes it will win my hand as his prize.'

Penelope's heart was heavy as she watched the jostling stream of vulgar suitors pick up the great bow and attempt to string it; but it grew lighter as the hours passed and, one after another, they all failed.

While the competition progressed, the door of the great hall was suddenly flung open, and a stranger walked in. He was tall and strongly built, but his beard was matted, his face filthy and his clothes were tattered rags. He went confidently towards the throne:

'I have come to try my hand at this contest.'

There was a burst of raucous laughter, a rumble of indignation tinged with menace. The stranger, ignoring this, strode straight to the great bow and picked it up.

Queen Penelope surveyed the unquiet scene wearily, beyond caring about the result. She shrugged and stood up, turning to Telemachus. 'Let this foolish bravado continue as long as it needs to,' she said. 'You, my son, shall judge it fairly. I shall be in my private quarters: bring me news there.'

So she went away and spent the night alone in her chamber, where she wept herself into a

*Penelope, the patient wife of Odysseus, weaves, while her violent and unruly suitors battle in the background.*
[British Library Royal MS 16 G.v, f.45v]

*Odysseus and his men burn out the drunken Cyclops' single eye.*
[British Library C.77.i.9, opp. p.113]

deep sleep. Then at dawn she was shaken awake by her faithful old maidservant.

'Mistress, Mistress, wake up! Last night . . . such things have happened! You must get up quickly and come. From this morning, you are a free and happy woman again!'

Penelope arose in amazement. Bewildered, she dressed and followed the maidservant out, hurrying to the hall. The rough band of men had all vanished; everything was cleared away and freshly washed; it was strangely silent. Only the ragged stranger sat there, waiting for her.

The servant whispered, 'There was a terrible battle in here last night, Mistress. Such bloodshed and violence: praise the gods you did not see it!' She shuddered. 'But look at this man, Mistress – surely you know him?'

Penelope did not answer.

The servant cried, 'But he is your own lord, Odysseus!'

Penelope, wide-eyed, turned to look at the stranger. He lifted his head and met her gaze.

'Last night, he strung the bow and shot the arrow straight home through the twelve axe-heads,' the servant went on. 'Then there was uproar, and your lord destroyed his rivals straight away: that crowd of foul men who have been harassing you for so long – they are all dead!'

Penelope could not speak: she could hardly breathe. She stared at the stranger, and could not believe that what she heard was true.

Softly he said, 'I am waiting for a welcome from my queen.'

Penelope answered carefully at last. 'You have certainly won the contest, my lord. But only yesterday you arrived, unannounced, from nowhere. Today, flushed with your recent victory, you suddenly claim a most unlikely identity. I think I am entitled at least to hear your story. Why should I believe you?'

The stranger stood up, holding her eyes with a wry smile. 'Oh Penelope, you have become a hard hearted woman!'

Reluctantly Penelope acknowledged that he bore a resemblance to her own beloved Odysseus. 'But I have spent twenty long years waiting for my husband to return,' she said, 'always on my guard against impostors. How should I know that you are who you say? If you really are Odysseus, tell me what has kept you away for so long?'

He replied, 'You know that the war in Troy lasted for all of ten years. You would have been deeply ashamed if I had abandoned my allies before it was won.'

Penelope was still incredulous. 'Another ten years have passed since then', she exclaimed. 'It is less than a month's voyage from Troy to Ithaca. If it is really you, Odysseus, if the love you profess for me is so strong, why did you not come straight home?'

Odysseus weighed his words cautiously before he spoke.

'The gods were against me from the beginning' he said. 'Firstly, they sent violent winds that blew my twelve ships far off course, to an unknown island whose people live solely upon lotus fruit. I allowed some of my men to taste this strange food – and as if by enchantment, at once they forgot everything, lost all desire for everything, even our journey home, wanting only to consume more and more of it. That was the first delay: I had to drag them back to the ships by force. But fortunately I myself did not taste any lotus; and Penelope, not once did I forget you.'

'Then we sailed on wherever the winds took us, until we came again to land. But this island held worse terrors, for it was inhabited by fearsome, one-eyed monsters called Cyclopes. One of them imprisoned us in his cave and killed and ate many of my men. The rest of us managed to escape when I tricked him into drunkenness and burnt out his single eye.

'We continued until we came to the island ruled by Aeolus, Lord of the Winds. Here I thought my luck would change, for on hearing our anxiety to return to Ithaca, he gathered up all the winds that might hinder us, tied them securely in a bag, and gave this into my safe-keeping. I stored it away carefully, telling no man what was in it. Then we made wonderful progress, until we could actually see the mountains of Ithaca on the horizon. I was overjoyed and allowed myself to fall into my first deep sleep since leaving Troy. Ah, Penelope, if only I had stayed watchful – I would have been back here with you many years ago. But while I slept, my jealous crew, believing I was hiding some great treasure from them, pulled out the bag of winds and opened it up. Of course, at once all the winds rushed out from their prison and blew up into a storm so fierce that I would not wish you even to imagine it. It lifted our ships into the air and smashed them down in a far, lonely corner of the ocean. Even worse was the land we found there, where we hoped to rest a little while. The country was inhabited by barbaric cannibal-giants who hurled rocks down the cliffs and destroyed eleven of my ships utterly, killing all their crews. Only my own vessel was left.'

Penelope was very still as she listened, betraying nothing of what she was thinking.

He went on, 'There is still much to tell. Devastated as we were, we survivors sailed on until we reached the island of Aeaea. This place is ruled by a powerful sorceress called Circe. As soon as my men came upon her palace, she transformed them into pigs and incarcerated them in her sty! Fortunately, the gods showed me a magic herb which enabled me to withstand her spells; and I persuaded her to return my men to their own shapes. After that, we remained resting and feasting in Circe's tranquil abode for a whole year.' He glanced aside, shaking his head. 'I cannot explain to you why.'

'I see,' said Penelope. 'And then?'

'And then Circe gave me some advice. She suggested that we sail beyond the edge of the mist, until we reached the Underworld, the realm of the dead. Overcoming our fear, we went there and searched through that dark land for the spirit of the blind prophet Teiresias. He alone, Circe said, could foresee the many dangers that still lay ahead of us, and tell me how best to overcome them. So we made the necessary sacrifices and watched the ghosts go by until at last Teiresias came. He told me how you were longing for me, Penelope, just as I was longing for you; and how your own suffering was parallel to my own. You cannot know what that meant to me. And he also warned me of the perils that lurked ahead: of the sirens – evil sea-witches whose heartbreakingly sweet songs lure men to certain death; and of the straits guarded by six-headed Scylla and her treacherous, death sucking partner Charybdis; and how to escape them. Finally we emerged unharmed from the Underworld, and navigated as we had been told, gradually coming closer to home. But then we reached the land that belongs to the Sun, and our fortune changed again.'

'Teiresias had warned us not to touch any of the Sun's cattle that grazed there. But my men were starving and ignored, or forgot, that wise advice. They killed some of the beasts and we all ate them. And so, within a few hours of setting sail again, we came into a mighty thunderstorm. The ship's mast was struck directly by lightning. Every last man drowned, except for me.'

'I clung to the broken mast, drifting in that way for nine whole days. When at last the waves threw me up onto a beach, I was half dead. On this unknown island I found myself in the care of a nymph called Calypso. She nursed my body back to health, but after such ordeals, my spirit was badly wounded. I could not come back to you like that. So I stayed there, waiting while it healed, for all of seven years.'

Penelope said, 'They say that nymphs are very beautiful and never grow old. No doubt this Calypso used her many charms to keep you there?'

'Of course, she was in love with me, Penelope; but all through those long years, my heart was tightly bound to yours. Finally I persuaded her that her love would be tainted if she kept me with her against my will. So she helped me to build a boat, and I set off once again for home.'

'But again I was ship-wrecked, again washed up on a beach half-dead, again rescued by a beautiful young woman – a king's daughter this time – who fell in love with me and begged me to marry her. As always, I refused. As soon as I was recovered, that king gave me a new ship and crew. This time, I crossed the sea safely and arrived home here, in Ithaca.'

'What more can I tell you, my only queen? I came straight to our palace in disguise. I proved myself the only master of this island, since only I had the power to string and shoot the king's bow. I destroyed all of your persecutors in a single night. After such a journey, such perils, such conquests, what else must I do to prove myself, before you will grant me the prize of your love?'

His voice was near to breaking as he finished. Morning had passed through noon, into evening. For a long time Penelope sat on in silence, gazing at nothing. Then she rose with a sigh and said,

'Your story is certainly extraordinary; but you cannot expect me to believe in it – or in you – without some proof. For two whole decades I have kept myself pure, always waiting for my husband. It would be the cruellest treachery, if now I were deceived into breaking that chastity by an impostor.'

'It is late,' she went on. 'Much has happened. We both need to refresh ourselves with sleep. I myself shall go to my private room.' Suddenly she looked at him sharply. 'But as a mark of respect for your achievements, I shall let you have the king's own bed tonight. My servants shall carry it out of the royal bedroom for you, now.'

At these words, he looked up in sudden agitation. 'The royal bed,' he cried. 'But that is impossible – unless – of course, you must be testing me! Penelope, I know that this bed can never be moved, am I not right? For one of the bedposts is an olive tree that is still alive and growing, rooted deeply into the ground. And that fact has always been a closely guarded secret, has it not?'

Penelope nodded. Now she was flushed like a rose, and suddenly began to tremble. He continued, 'No one ever knew about this, except for yourself, Penelope, a single faithful servant, and . . .?'

'And Odysseus,' she whispered. 'There, concealed within that insignificant secret, you have found the key to your proof, Odysseus. And now, with my whole heart, I can welcome you home.'

# The Tale of Cupid and Psyche

The tale of Cupid and Psyche first appears as a story within a story in the *Metamorphoses* of Lucius Apuleius, popularly known as 'The Golden Ass'. Written in the second century AD, *The Golden Ass* is a series of linked stories told in the first person, describing how the hero Lucius, because of his insatiable curiosity about magic, is transformed into an ass, while keeping his human mind. In his search for the antidote, which is to eat roses, he is stolen by robbers and suffers many adventures and misfortunes before regaining his human shape with the aid of the goddess Isis.

Apuleius was born *c*.AD 123–5 at Madaurus, a Roman colony of North Africa. He was educated at Carthage and Athens, and subsequently pleaded in the law courts at Rome. After travelling extensively he returned to North Africa, to what is now Tripoli, where he was accused of murder and practising magic. The first charge was dropped and he defended himself successfully against the second. He returned to Carthage, where he enjoyed fame as a poet, philosopher and public speaker. He became chief priest of the province and was an initiate of the mysteries of Isis.

In Apuleius' tale the story of Cupid and Psyche is told by an old woman to a young girl, who has been captured by robbers, to keep her spirits up. The story echoes that of *The Golden Ass* as a whole and has been described as 'a fairy-tale version of Lucius' experiences'. Both Lucius and Psyche are undone by their curiosity, and Psyche's subsequent wanderings and trials have been compared to Lucius' misfortunes while in the body of the ass. Both are eventually redeemed by divine intervention. By telling the story in the form of a myth Apuleius is giving a more universal meaning to Lucius' experiences.

There has been much scholarly debate about the origins of the Cupid and Psyche story. It has been considered variously to be legend, fairy-tale, allegory or myth – or some combination of these. Folklorists have found countless variations on the theme in many parts of the world, and suggest Apuleius took an existing folk-tale as the basis of his story, adding to it the names of characters from mythology. Similarities can be seen with such well-known stories as *Blue Beard*, *Beauty and the Beast* and *Cinderella*.

It is regarded by some as a philosophical myth with Cupid and Psyche representing Love and the

*Border from an illuminated page of a copy of the first printed edition of*
The Golden Ass, *1469, with a portrait of Apuleius.*
[British Library G.8997]

24

Soul, related to Plato's account of the pilgrimage of the soul in *Phaedrus*. Another view is that Apuleius adapted an existing myth, but this is not supported by any surviving ancient works of art. Although representations of Cupid and Psyche dating back to at least the fourth century BC exist, they do not appear to relate to any of the incidents in Apuleius' work. Other suggestions are that it is an adaptation or re-working of an existing work of fiction which has not survived, possibly of Greek origin, or that it is a fictional account of the initiation rites into the mysteries of Isis.

Since its composition *The Golden Ass* and particularly the tale of Cupid and Psyche has been a major source of inspiration for many forms of literature and art. Saint Augustine of Hippo (345–430) was clearly familiar with *The Golden Ass*, as is apparent from discussions in his works. In the sixth century Fulgentius composed a long Christian allegorical interpretation. It is possible that a story in Geoffrey of Monmouth's *Historia regum Britanniae* written in the twelfth century is based on the tale of Cupid and Psyche. There are also French romances that suggest that the story was known in the Middle Ages.

It was, however, from the fourteenth century onwards with the dawn of the Renaissance that interest in Apuleius' work really awakened. This was largely due to Giovanni Boccaccio (1313?–75), the Italian novelist and poet, who discovered and copied a manuscript of *The Golden Ass*. His latin treatise *De Genealogia Deorum* (Genealogy of the Gods) includes a re-telling of the story of Cupid and Psyche. Boccaccio's work in turn made the story known and inspired many other different literary treatments. The first printing of Apuleius' work in Rome in 1469 and the first translation into English in 1566 gave added impetus to the popularity of the story, both on the continent and in England. Edmund Spenser alludes to the tale in *The Faerie Queen* (1590), and in 1636 Thomas Heywood produced a dramatic interpretation *Loves Mistris, or the Queens Masque*, which was highly successful. Other distinguished versions of the story have been a drama by Molière produced in Paris in 1671 and *Les Amours de Psyche et Cupidon* by Jean de la Fontaine, a mixture of prose and poetry, published in 1669.

In the nineteenth century many poets made use of the story: amongst them John Keats, who wrote an 'Ode to Psyche' and William Morris, who included the tale in his long poetic work *The Earthly Paradise*. An attractive prose version is that of Walter Pater which he included in his novel *Marius the Epicurean* in 1885. Since the end of that century *The Golden Ass*, and particularly the tale of Cupid and Psyche, has been a popular text with private presses and there are many finely printed editions. Twentieth-century interest has tended to focus more on the psychological aspects of the story. Amongst Greek myths probably *Oedipus* alone has received more attention in this field.

Often allied to the dramatic uses of the story have been musical works. Over the centuries there have been numerous operas and ballets, and in recent times composers such as César Franck, Claude Debussy and Paul Hindemith have written works inspired by the subject. Many artists have recognised the pictorial qualities of the story and there have been numerous renderings from the fourteenth century onwards. Images of Cupid and Psyche still epitomise romantic love; for example, many representations of them are to be found on Valentine's Day cards.

*Venus, jealous of Psyche's great beauty, instructs Cupid to cause her to fall in love with a monstrous creature.*
[British Library C.105.g.6]

A KING and queen had three daughters. The two eldest had a choice of admirers, and so married as soon as they came of age. However, the youngest princess, Psyche, was so unusually beautiful and sweet-natured that people whispered she was surely divine; and although she was much admired, no man considered himself worthy enough to seek her hand in marriage.

Rumours about Psyche travelled and grew. They reached the ears of Venus, goddess of love, and gnawed at her heart. Venus called up her son, Cupid, and commanded him to punish this upstart beauty by matching her to a foul and unwholesome lover.

Time passed. The king and queen, despairing of ever finding Psyche a husband, consulted an oracle of Apollo. The message that came back to them struck horror into their hearts:

*Lead the girl to the mountain top*
*where the unseen monster lurks.*
*He will take her for his bride.*

They wept together, and debated whether to risk opposing the gods' will. But Psyche, anticipating no meaningful future without a husband, agreed to accept the hideous creature chosen for her. Grieving, the king and queen took her up the mountain and left her there to wait for him, alone.

Out of the loneliness, Zephyrus the West Wind blew up softly. He carried the girl far away to a valley carpeted with soft grass and sheltered by trees. Within it stood a magnificent palace. The door was open: Psyche went in.

Nobody came to meet her. But every room was filled with rich furnishings, delicious food and soft strains of music; invisible voices called upon her to partake of the luxuries within.

So Psyche helped herself to fruits, honey and sweetmeats, and refreshed herself in the palace fountains. Then night began to fall. She found a bedchamber, and lay down.

No lamps were lit. No moon or stars shone outside the window. Soon the darkness thickened, until it was impenetrable, complete.

And in the darkness – suddenly, someone was there! She had heard no footsteps. No door opened. Where had he come from, what was he like? There was no time to be afraid: almost at once, her unseen husband was making her gasp at the strength of his love.

She asked him, 'Who are you?'

A soft laugh answered her.

'Why can't I see you?'

'I am supposed to be your punishment.'

In the darkness, she put out a hand, trying to make sense of his shape. 'Are you really a monster?'

'Ask no questions, Psyche. I promise I will come to you each night, and make you happy. By day, this whole palace and the forest around it, are for your own comfort and delight. Trust in me, and nothing will go wrong.'

PSYCHE BORNE OFF BY ZE-
PHYRUS, DRAWN BY EDWARD
BURNE-JONES & ENGRAVED
BY WILLIAM MORRIS

So Psyche settled into her new life. It was strange, but not unhappy. For a while she asked no questions and made no trouble. But by and by she grew lonely, and begged her unseen husband to let her see her family. At last he reluctantly gave in, and arranged for her two sisters to visit her.

They were astonished when Zephyrus carried them to the secret dwelling – and outraged when they heard that Psyche had never seen the creature who made love to her each night.

'But he's so good to me,' Psyche insisted. 'I have everything I want here, and more. In return he only asks me to trust him.'

'It's a sham!' they retorted. 'You must face up to it, Psyche: you've been married off to a monster. The gods themselves said so! This creature is fattening you up to devour you!'

By the time the sisters were taken home, they had tormented Psyche with doubts. Her heart wanted to trust the love she now felt for her husband; but her head insisted, it was only reasonable to know the truth, to give herself a chance to escape while she could.

So, full of misgivings, she found a lamp and hid it underneath the marital bed. That night, when her husband lay in the deep sleep of contented love, she drew it out and lit it.

*Psyche discovers the identity of the sleeping Cupid.*
[British Library C.99.b.32]

In the flickering yellow light she caught her breath. She saw – not some foul, misshapen creature – but a handsome young man whose features and lithe body were as perfect in every way as her own. But he was no mortal youth, for behind his back lay a folded pair of wings!

As she gazed at this god, Psyche's hand began to tremble uncontrollably, so that a drop of hot oil spilt from the lamp onto his shoulder. He cried out in pain, and sat up.

For the first time, their eyes met. But the god's clouded with seething anger, until Psyche was forced to look away.

'So: now you know me.' His voice was empty.

And Psyche whispered, still trembling, 'Cupid. The lord of love!'

*Psyche, abandoned to her fate on the mountain-top, is rescued and carried away by Zephyrus, the West Wind.*
[British Library C.43.c.16]

'But you have broken my love now, Psyche, broken it into a thousand shards. I tried to save you from a cruel fate, but, because you would not trust me, my mother will discover I have deceived her. She hates you, Psyche, because your beauty is equal to hers. She will force me to abandon you, and keep us apart. You have lost everything! I am torn from you – I shall never be able to come back!'

And before she could murmur her remorse, Cupid had spread his shimmering wings and vanished into the night.

\* \* \*

Psyche felt she had destroyed her whole being: she wanted to kill herself. As dawn came up, she ran to the deepest part of the forest and flung herself into the great river that flowed through it. But the spirits of the waters carried her gently to the far bank, and washed her in a healing sleep.

When she awoke, she realised it was her destiny to carry on living. She rose and began to wander aimlessly through the trees, while her thoughts darted here and there, like butterflies. But whichever way they turned, they always came back to the same point: *Love. Cupid. Love.*

'I must search until I find him,' she said to herself. 'That will give my life meaning, and that is the meaning of my life.'

Hours passed, days passed, months passed. Psyche wandered through the world, always searching. She came out of the forest, to villages and towns; and then into wilder places where the steep slopes were covered with bare rocks. Her purpose was like a bright light within her: neither misery nor hardship could extinguish it.

By and by, she came to a temple, and found – with a mixture of joy and trepidation – that it was dedicated to Cupid's mother, the jealous goddess Venus.

Psyche entered the cool, fragrant gloom and humbly made her offering. Soon, a voice came to her:

'Foul girl! Bewitcher of my son, blight upon my own beauty! What do you want of me?'

'Holy Venus, I humbly beg you: please send me back my husband!'

A cruel peal of laughter echoed inside her head: 'No-one can achieve their heart's desire unless they work for it.'

'I am not too proud . . .'

'No, but you will prove to be too feeble! Nevertheless, here is a task: go to the granary behind my temple. Inside it, you will see a great heap of grain: wheat and barley, beans and millett. You must sort it all into separate piles, with not a single grain in the wrong place. It must be done by nightfall!'

*Psyche visits the Underworld, and other tasks imposed upon her by Venus.*
[British Library 241.b.11]

Psyche held her head high as she went out, but when she looked inside the granary, she saw at once that the task was impossible.

But unknown to her, far away, Cupid (a prisoner of his own pride as much as his mother's envy) was watching Psyche, every moment of every day. Now, secretly, he called up a whole tribe of ants to help her. They came swarming into the granary and skilfully, efficiently, sorted all the grains.

At sunset, the ants left. Then Venus came in person, and found the impossible task completed. Suspicion flashed from her eyes: she would not give up her son.

The next morning she said, 'Go down to the meadow, wretch. Take this sack, and fill it with wool from the golden sheep that graze there.'

Psyche ran there eagerly; but when she reached the meadow gate, she saw that the sheep were all vicious rams with horns as sharp as spears; they stood ready to charge, and gore her to death.

However, at the bottom of the meadow was a stream, and beside it grew a great drift of reeds. As she hesitated, these reeds began to bend and moan and murmur, until she made out a voice calling to her: 'Look in the hedges, Psyche, where the golden wool has caught on the sharp thorns: fill your sack from there!'

Psyche looked, saw that it was true, and began at once to gather the wool. Though her fingers were badly scratched at the end of the day, no other harm came to her, and she was able to present Venus with a sack from which the golden wool was overflowing.

Venus was neither grateful nor impressed, but beside herself with rage. From under her robes she produced a small casket and pushed it into Psyche's hands.

'Take this,' she hissed, 'and carry it to the realm of shadows and death – the Underworld! *If* you manage to find your way there (if Cerberus the watchdog lets you pass his blood-lusting fangs, and if you are not swept away by the voracious waters of the River Styx), you must seek out the goddess Persephone. Give her this box and beg her to put into it a few droplets of her own beauty. Tell her it is because my own looks have been faded by the trouble *you* have brought me.'

Silently, Psyche took the box and turned away. But when the goddess was out of sight, she threw herself to the ground and began to cry hysterically. This was truly impossible! No mortal could ever reach the Underworld, except through death itself. Again, Psyche's thoughts turned to suicide.

But then other thoughts (or was it a voice?) crowded in on her: 'Do not give up! Walk until you come to a cave. Enter it and go on, into the shadows. Be brave! Do not fear Cerberus, but speak to him gently: he will let you pass. When you reach the banks of the Styx wait there: in time you will hear the ferryman's oars approaching. If you pay him with more sweet words, he will carry you safely all the way. Nothing is impossible! But do not meddle with the box.'

So Psyche sighed, got up and forced herself to follow the formless voice. Everything happened as it had promised. She found the cave, calmed the watchdog, charmed the grim-faced ferryman, and drifted through the blindness of shadows until she found Persephone. That goddess smiled kindly at her, for she too was young and burdened with sorrows of her own. She filled Venus' box with something secret, and hastily sent Psyche away.

So Psyche returned, and trudged back to the temple. Surely now Venus would relent?

She sat down and fell into a daydream, remembering Cupid's love. She had been so immaculate then . . . but now (she gazed down at herself in disgust) — now her shapely body was deformed by hunger and her long quest. Cupid would surely be repelled.

And yet inside this box . . . No, she must not touch it! But if she could only borrow just a tiny drop of Persephone's essence of beauty — just a little — so that Venus would not notice . . .

Very carefully, she prised open the lid.

At once, a fragrant, intoxicating mist burst out. It wafted over her eyes, clung to her body, wrapped her whole weary being in a soft blanket of sleep . . .

Venus was not waiting for her: she did not expect her return. But Cupid, watching everything, could contain his passion no longer. He broke free of his imprisonment, and flew straight to Psyche with the speed of a gale. He woke her, rebuked her for succumbing to curiosity again, and returned the secret substance to the casket. Then he urged her onwards, to his mother's temple.

Venus was astonished to see Psyche still alive, bringing the gift she lusted after. She snatched the casket greedily and waved Psyche away, muttering half formed words of forgiveness.

Cupid, meanwhile, had flown straight to Heaven and poured out Psyche's story to Lord Jupiter. The high god listened, and was moved. He sent his messenger to bring Psyche to him at once.

Now Psyche had grown from a lovely, half-formed innocent, through error and anguish, through faith and fortitude, until she was whole, complete. Jupiter ruled that she was to become immortal, and to wallow in the radiance of love which every pure soul longs for.

So Cupid and Psyche were properly joined in Heaven. From then on they lived with the gods; and their child was called Delight.

# The Legendary Journeys of Alexander the Great

Even as Alexander the Great (born 356 BC; died 323 BC), the son of Philip II of Macedon and Olympias of Epirus, fought his way across Asia, his story was being written. From 335 BC until his execution by Alexander in 327 BC on the charge of conspiracy, Aristotle's nephew, Callisthenes of Olynthus, was composing the eye-witness history of the campaign in Asia. Soon after Alexander's death, Aristobulus, a Greek engineer, Chares of Mitylene and Ptolemy, afterwards founder of the Ptolemaic dynasty in Egypt, wrote of the events in which they had taken part in close association with their Macedonian leader. Other participants, such as Alexander's fleet commander, Nearchus of Lato, and chief helmsman, Onesicratus of Astypaleia, wrote up particular episodes in the campaign. 'So many writers of his deeds did Alexander the Great have with him' marvelled the Roman orator Cicero.

Although only a few fragments of these and other contemporary texts survive, five full accounts of Alexander's life by the later classical authors from the Roman period – Diodorus of Sicily, Pompeius Trogus, Plutarch, Arrian and Quintus Curtius – draw their information from these earlier literary sources. In addition the *Romance of Alexander* (frequently referred to as Pseudo-Callisthenes, after an erroneous late attribution to Alexander's official historian) preserves many stories concerning Alexander that grew up soon after his death. It is to these six texts that subsequent generations owe their knowledge of Alexander.

Yet not only was it the case that, as Strabo remarked, 'All who wrote about Alexander preferred the marvellous to the true'; readers also preferred to hear marvellous tales about Alexander. From late antiquity onwards the *Romance*, which continued to embellish its narrative with further strands of imaginative fiction, became the principal and frequently the sole source of knowledge about Alexander. Originally written in Greek, the Alexander *Romance* soon spawned version after version, in virtually every known language; from India to Spain and from Iceland to Ethiopia it enthralled readers with tales of Alexander's far-ranging conquests and curious adventures.

In western Europe during the medieval period, numerous Latin and vernacular versions of Pseudo-Callisthenes were written. Among the most important of these was the ninth-century abbreviation, or *Epitome*, of Julius Valerius' fourth-century *Res Gestae Alexandri Macedonis* ('The Deeds of Alexander of Macedon'), which is itself a descendant of one of the earliest versions of Pseudo-Callisthenes. The very first French verse romance based on a classical subject, the *Roman d'Alexandre* ('Romance of Alexander') written by Alexandre de Bernai around 1185, derives from the *Epitome*. The accounts given of Alexander

*Olympias gives birth to Alexander the Great. Portents of his future greatness include the two eagles that appeared on the roof of his father's palace and were said to foretell Alexander's two empires in Europe and Asia; also the burning down of the temple at Ephesus, which occurred in the same year as Alexander's birth, but was subsequently said to have occurred on the same day and to portend his revenge on the Persians for their earlier invasion of Greece under Xerxes.*
[British Library Royal MS 20 C.iii, f.15]

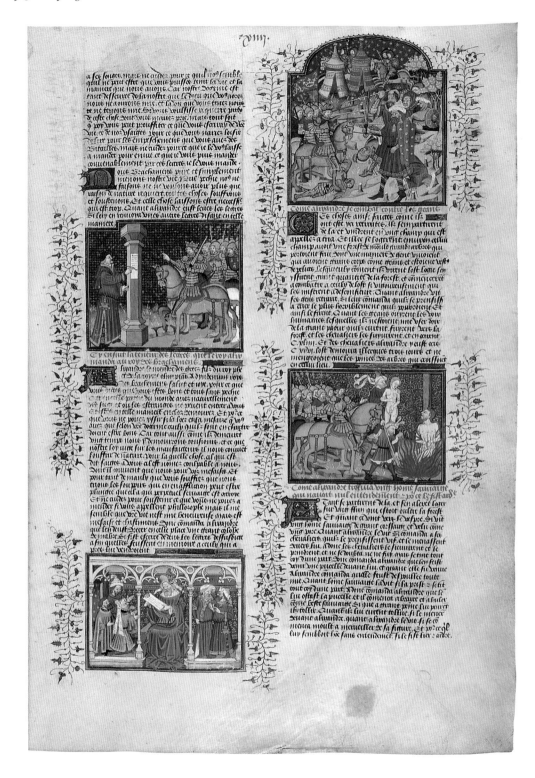

in the earliest vernacular world chronicle, the *Histoire ancienne jusqu'à César* ('Ancient history before Caesar'), and Vincent de Beauvais's encyclopaedia, the *Speculum historiale* ('Mirror of History') are also based on Julius Valerius. Another version of Pseudo-Callisthenes that was brought to the West from Constantinople around 950 and first translated into Latin shortly afterwards gave rise to the highly influential *Historia de Preliis* ('History of Battles') and an important vernacular text of the thirteenth century, now known as the *Old French Prose Alexander Romance*.

Perhaps as early as the sixth century, the same early version of the *Romance* that gave rise to Julius Valerius produced, in the Christian Orient, the Armenian Alexander Romance. The other version that reached the West in the tenth century had already been translated into Syriac by the sixth century and subsequently formed the source of other eastern versions of the story. Most notably this Syriac text influenced the account of Alexander given in the Qur'an (in which he appears as Dhu'l-Quarnyn or The Two-Horned One) and in the Persian poetical epic, the *Shah-Nama* (Book of Kings) by the tenth-century poet Firdawsi, in which Alexander is incorporated into the Persian king-lists as a son of Darius II. Firdawsi's treatment of the story in turn influenced such later Persian poets as the twelfth-century author Nizami in his *Iskandar-nama*, part of his *Khamsa* or Quintet of poems. The Syriac text also travelled to Ethiopia, where it was again translated for eastern Christian readers.

From the thirteenth until the end of the fifteenth century western artists lavishly illustrated manuscripts containing Latin and vernacular versions of the *Romance*. Typical of such illustrations are those of Alexander ascending into the heavens in a cage supported by winged griffins and descending into depths of the sea in a glass barrel [*see* jacket illustration, and on pages 38 and 40].

From the fifteenth until as late as the nineteenth century some of the most accomplished Persian and Mughal artists produced beautifully illustrated copies of the *Shah-Nama* and *Khamsa* that included many episodes from their distinctive account of the life of Alexander (or Iskandar as he was known in the Islamic world). In these we see, for example, Alexander consulting the wise Brahmins (the 'Gymnosophists' or 'Naked Philosophers' of the Romance (opposite) and also the Water of Life through which the hero hoped to achieve immortality.

Such a man as Alexander was obviously bound to have a significant and wide-ranging legacy. His military conquests embraced over half the known world and are still unequalled. His continual success and apparently limitless energy demand respect. Not only have his achievements persistently inspired awe in subsequent generations; the motivating force behind his relentless progress far beyond the familiar and known world of civilised Greece has been the object of fascinated speculation. For the western medieval reader he became the archetype of human ambition. In clerical hands such ambition inevitably reached too far and came into conflict with the will of God; thus Alexander's ascent into the heavens is halted by the hand of the Almighty. For a powerful noble such aspirations were an attractive model. In the Islamic world Alexander's motivation was quickly interpreted as a spiritual one – an inward journey in search of wisdom and the very immortality which he and his immediate successors had claimed for him.

*Scenes from the Romance of Alexander: on the left Alexander exchanges letters with Dindimus, the leader of the ascetic Brahmans of India, on the merits of their very different lifestyles; on the right Alexander fights with a race of giants, dressed in oriental style, and orders the burning of man who has been judged a savage, on account of his animal-like reaction to a naked girl placed before him.*
[British Library Royal MS 15 E.vi, f.18]

*Alexander rises into the heavens carried upwards in a wooden cage by four griffins who fly up to reach the meat on the end of two stakes held aloft by Alexander.*
[British Library Royal MS 15 E.vi, f.20v]

## KING ALEXANDER OF MACEDONIA

liberator of the Greek nations, conqueror of half of Asia,
emperor of Greece and Persia.
Born at Pella in 356 BC.
Died at Babylon in 323 BC aged 32.

ALEXANDER'S most significant achievement was his conquest of the Persian Empire. He is also remembered for his relentless march eastward through Asia, at the head of a vast army, culminating in the conquest of India; and the twelve cities founded in his name, especially Alexandria-in-Egypt.

Alexander was a unique and charismatic man. Having acceded to monarchy, power and heavy responsibility at an early age, he complemented his superb military skills with cunning diplomacy and nobility of spirit. An inherently restless figure, his key motivations were the desire to explore unknown foreign lands and his quest for immortality.

He was born at Pella in Macedonia, the only child of King Philip and Queen Olympias. However, his childhood was clouded by doubts about his true paternity: it is said that his real father was the queen's court magician Nectanebo, the last Pharaoah of Egypt, who tricked Olympias into an affair by disguising himself as the god, Ammon. Nevertheless, Alexander was accepted by Philip as the royal heir, and given a fitting education by the philosopher Aristotle.

He was an unusual looking youth: notably small of stature and afflicted by a squint; but his hair and general demeanour were widely described as lion-like. His talents and forceful personality were soon apparent: whilst still a schoolboy, he frequently organised his fellow students into mock battle manoeuvres, always choosing to give intelligent advice and encouragement to the losing side. He also displayed an uncanny mastery over animals: at the age of 15 he effortlessly tamed his father's ferocious horse Bucephalus, retaining it as his official mount and constant companion throughout his life.

Following the murder of his father in 336 BC Alexander found himself crowned king of Macedonia. For some time he had nurtured a growing rancour against Darius, Emperor of Persia, who had forced Philip and neighbouring Greek kings to pay him vast annual tributes. Even before he was crowned, Alexander had audaciously refused to accede to the demands of Darius' ambassadors: declining to provide the gold demanded, he had sent threatening messages instead. Now almost his first act was to declare war against Persia, with the intention of freeing his people from the slavery of colonial status. Such was the draw of his personality that 70,000 men volunteered to join his army of liberation, including many ageing veterans whom the youthful monarch called up in order to benefit from their greater experience.

The route he took from Macedonia to Persia led him through many city-states, subduing each in turn by either diplomatic persuasion or military might. The vanquished peoples voted him king of all Greece, putting a vast resource of men and weaponry at his disposal.

*Alexander's descent into the sea in a glass diving bell. His queen and her lover attempt to drown him by cutting the chains that support him. Alexander is subsequently saved by knowing that if he kills the cat which accompanies him, the sea, which cannot tolerate blood, will throw the bell and its contents onto dry land.*
[British Library Royal MS 20 B.xx, f.77v]

Exhilarated by his seemingly unstoppable success, Alexander led his troops on to what he then regarded as his ultimate confrontation: with the despised King Darius of Persia. Their first encounter was through an exchange of letters, in which Darius attempted to humiliate Alexander by mocking his youth and branding him a mere terrorist: Alexander rejoined with dignity. The decisive battle between the armies of Greece and Persia took place shortly afterwards, at Issus on the coast of Syria. The Greek victory was all the more remarkable for the previous invincibility of the opposing side. Darius' equipment, wife, daughters and mother were all captured by the Greeks; however the Persian emperor himself escaped, to Alexander's considerable chagrin.

Having conquered Greater Armenia, Alexander now led his troops to the river

Euphrates, building an iron bridge to cross into Persia, and then immediately dismantling it to discourage deserters. Following this, the Greek and re-formed Persian armies met in the bloody battle of Arbela, whose conclusion was postponed by a Persian retreat to replenish their supplies. The Greeks pursued them, using various tricks devised by Alexander to fuel the enemy's growing unease. When the fighting resumed, the Greeks were the definitive victors. Darius escaped yet again, only to be murdered shortly afterwards by two of his own viceroys, Bessus and Nabarzanes. By chance, Alexander is said to have arrived on the scene just as Darius was dying. In a typical display of Alexander's generous character, the two leaders affected an extraordinary reconciliation, with Darius granting his daughter Roxane to Alexander in marriage.

Alexander's main ambition was already achieved, and he now turned his attention to the administration of his new empire. However, it was soon apparent that victory had not cured his perennial restlessness. He was also becoming increasingly fearful of his own ultimate destiny and doom. Shortly after his marriage, it is said that he disappeared into the wilderness for several months with a small band of faithful troops. He subsequently described his adventures in a long letter to his mother. His writings described fantastical travels through unmapped regions, varying from the desolate to the inordinately fruitful; and encounters with giants, three-eyed lions, flame-shooting birds, headless men, disembodied voices and other mysterious creatures. The letter reveals his desire to find the end of the earth itself: on one occasion he descended in a glass barrel to the bottom of the sea; on another, he claimed to have flown almost to heaven in a cage raised up by four griffins. He also described his arrival at the dark 'Land of the Blessed' where one of his subordinates inadvertently discovered the 'Water of Life': Alexander, however, failed to taste this even though it might perhaps have averted his untimely death.

After this interlude Alexander seemed revitalised in his urge to travel yet further and achieve new conquests. His goal now was India. At this point a large body of his men attempted to mutiny, but were pacified by Alexander's phenomenal powers of persuasion. As with Darius, his initial encounter with King Porus of India comprised an exchange of insulting letters. Porus then despatched his army of elephants and other wild beasts to terrify the Greeks: Alexander successfully repelled them with a wall of red-hot metal. The conventional battle which followed lasted for twenty days, after which Greek morale had diminished so severely that Alexander was forced to contemplate the possibility of his first ever defeat. Having more faith in himself than his men, he proposed to Porus that final victory should be decided by single combat between the two leaders. It seemed an exceptionally risky challenge: Porus was a towering man, eight-feet tall, whilst Alexander was a bare five-feet. However, as they faced each other Porus was distracted by a noise: startled, he turned round, enabling Alexander to knock his legs from under him, and kill him with a single sword-blow. He then had the foresight to immediately grant the vanquished Indian troops their freedom, thus denying them any opportunity to undermine his simple victory with their obviously superior strength.

This was Alexander's last battle, and the climax of his military journeys and campaigns. It was followed by a further period of wandering through unknown lands, during which he sought

*Iskandar (Alexander) confers with the seven sages before setting out across the Western sea.*
[British Library Or. MS 6810, f.214]

*Iskandar (Alexander) visits the sage at night.*
[British Library Add. MS 27261, f.230]

meetings with many unusual people. The most notable of these were the Brahmans, naked philosophers who, it is recorded, slaked Alexander's thirst for wisdom in some enigmatic debates. He was much moved by their pacifism and by their reasoned disparagement of kingship and human aggression; nevertheless, he refused to be persuaded away from the insatiable quest for wordly glory, to which he believed 'Providence' had irrevocably assigned him. Having returned and set the affairs of his Indian colony in order, he then visited the fabled Sanctuary of the Sun and Moon. Here it is said that the oracle, in the form of two miraculous talking trees, predicted that his own death was imminent.

Profoundly disturbed by this revelation, he retreated to Persia, diverting en route through the spectacular 'Crystal Country' to the palace of Queen Candace of Meroe. Here he was

*Alexander consults the miraculous Trees of the Sun and the Moon, which foretell his early death.*
[British Library Add. MS 15268, f.214]

temporarily taken prisoner, but escaped by cunning negotiation. He also claimed to have visited the 'dwelling place of the gods' where he received the promise of enduring posthumous fame; and the land of the Amazons, 27,000 armed virgins living entirely without male company. Further travels described in letters to his mother took in the gold and silver Pillars of Heracles; the River Antlas and other lands beyond the Red Sea, inhabited by weird semi-human beasts; the City of the Sun; and the sapphire temple of Lyssos, and the palace of Cyrus the Great. Throughout these journeys he continued to be haunted by unfortunate omens and prophesies of impending doom.

Alexander's last resting place was Babylon, where he was poisoned by Iolaus, one of his own cup-bearers. Enduring a long and agonisingly painful death with fortitude, he continued to display his customary wisdom, justice and humanity until the very end.

# The Seven Voyages of Sindbad the Sailor

Sindbad the Sailor appears in the great compilation of eastern stories known as 'A Thousand and One Nights' or more popularly as 'The Arabian Nights', though it may originally have been an independent work. It is a series of seven tales enclosed within a framework, which together form an artistic whole. The frame story consists of the wealthy merchant, Sindbad the Sailor, recounting the seven fantastic voyages he has made to an impoverished porter, Sindbad the Landsman, who has stopped to rest outside his mansion and is invited in. Their shared name highlights the contrast in their situations. After listening to the first story, Sindbad the Landsman is invited back on successive nights to marvel at the rest. At the end he acknowledges Sindbad the Sailor deserves his riches because of all the hardships he has endured.

Each of the seven voyages begins with a disaster – a shipwreck or other calamity. Sindbad is then faced with a series of adventures and encounters with monsters, some extremely perilous, some less so. Having extricated himself from danger, often using great cunning, he amasses a fortune, is rescued, usually the sole survivor of the voyage, and returns home a rich man, until the lure of the sea and adventure entice him on his next journey.

The earliest known fragment of the 'Arabian Nights' dates from the ninth century, but it almost certainly drew on older collections of stories and folk-tales. The earliest stories probably came from India and Persia, but there are many traces of ancient Egyptian, Greek and Roman tales to be found amongst them. The collection was probably translated into Arabic around the eighth century, with Arabic stories added soon afterwards. The 'Sindbad the Sailor' cycle of stories is believed to be of Arabic origin, probably originating in Baghdad or the sea-port of Basra between the end of the ninth and the beginning of the tenth centuries.

As early as the eighteenth century a work was published speculating as to the possible sources of the 'Sindbad' stories. Richard Hole in *Remarks on the Arabian Nights' Entertainments*, 1797, describes the stories as an 'Arabian Odyssey'. He saw similarities between the voyages and Homer's epic, particularly noting the correspondence of the cannibal giant in the third voyage with the Cyclops Polyphemus in the *Odyssey*. He also noted that many of the fantastic creatures described by Sindbad are to be found in the works of Pliny and Solinus.

The stories that make up Sindbad's voyages are a mixture of fact and fantastic fiction based on travellers' tales and sailors' yarns. Many of the descriptions and incidents can also be found in early Arab geographical works. The relation of marvels and wonders or *'aja'ib* was a distinct genre of literature in medieval Arab countries. Works such as al-Qazwini's 'Wonders of Creation' (*'Aja'ib al-Makhluqat*) of the thirteenth century relate many of the same wonders encountered by Sindbad on his journeys, and they probably shared a common source.

Sindbad's adventures are also paralleled in some early fictional accounts of travels from other countries and also in purportedly factual accounts such as those of Sir John de Mandeville and Marco Polo. An Egyptian Twelfth Dynasty papyrus, 'The Tale of the Shipwrecked Man' pre-figures some

*Sindbad the sailor entertains Sindbad the Landsman with stories of his voyages.*
[British Library K.T.C.102.b.2]

45

*A ship-wrecked sailor is rescued by a giant bird.*
[British Library Or. MS 12220, f.72v]

incidents from 'Sindbad' and in the second century AD Lucian in his 'True History' relates stories very similar to those of the roc's egg in Sindbad's fifth voyage, and the ship swallowed by the whale in one of the two versions of the seventh voyage. The sailors' mistaking of the back of a whale for an island is reminiscent of a similar incident in the 'Navigation of St Brendan', and several of the incidents also appear in a twelfth-century German romance *Herzog Ernst*.

These similarities probably reflect common oral traditions amongst sea-faring nations and the fact that the writers of '*aja'ib* borrowed not only from nautical yarns but also from the literature of antiquity: thus incidents from the *Odyssey* and the Alexander legends are echoed in the adventures of Sindbad.

The stories of 'The Arabian Nights' were first brought to the attention of European readers by the French scholar Antoine Galland (1646–1715). Galland acquired an isolated manuscript of 'Sindbad' in the 1690s. He subsequently obtained a Syrian manuscript of the 'Nights', and his translation of this was published between 1703 and 1717, to immense acclaim. He included 'Sindbad' although there is no proof that it ever formed part of the original Arabic version of the 'Nights'.

The first versions in English were translations of Galland with individual stories such as 'Sindbad' often circulating as cheap pamphlets. In 1839–41 the Reverend Edward Lane published his translation of many of the stories which proved very popular, but suffered from being heavily expurgated. The best known translation into English is probably that of Sir Richard Burton (1821–90) the scholar, diplomat and explorer. His work, published in 1885–8 is actually heavily indebted to the earlier work of John Payne (1842–1906). Where Lane had bowdlerised the text to conform to strict Victorian ideas of morality, Burton dwelt on and exaggerated its obscenities.

'Sindbad' is best known today through versions for children. The text was being cut to protect the young as early as the late eighteenth century, but it was towards the end of the nineteenth century that large numbers of selections from, and abridgements of, the 'Nights' started to appear, generally lavishly illustrated. Developments in printing led to the sumptuous coloured illustrations of the early twentieth century by artists such as Edmund Dulac and E. J. Detmold, and 'Sindbad' continues to be one of the most popular and frequently told tales from the collection.

Pantomime versions of 'Sindbad' are not often seen today, but were immensely popular in the nineteenth century. It was first presented as *The Valley of Diamonds, or, Harlequin Sindbad* at Drury Lane in 1814, and was followed by many extremely spectacular and lavish productions later in the century. There have been various cinematic versions of the 'Nights' and *The Seventh Voyage of Sinbad* was released in 1958 followed by several other film accounts of his voyages.

The American author John Barth's complex novels, of which *The Last Voyage of Somebody the Sailor* (1991) owes most to 'Sindbad', are in a long tradition of literature influenced by the 'Nights'. Edgar Allan Poe wrote a short story 'The Thousand-and-Second Tale of Scheherazade' which took Sindbad into the nineteenth century and presented him with wonders such as the telegraph.

MY dear friend, you must understand that this comfortable house in which we now sit, the exquisite foods, the sumptuous cushions, the beautiful slave-girls . . . such luxuries have not always been mine. It is true that, by the grace of Allah (praise be upon Him), I was born into such an agreeable style of life; but I confess that, in my youth I became a scoundrel and a wastrel, and frittered all my inheritance away. In the end I was reduced to such poverty that, with my last few coins, I bought myself passage upon a merchant ship, hoping that adventure on the boundless ocean might bring me some happy turn of fortune.

*The First Voyage*
We had only briefly been upon the sea when we reached what seemed to be an island: a place of lush forests, sweet-scented flowers and a dazzling profusion of colourful birds. Here I alighted and wandered about freely with some of the crew, making fires of driftwood upon the beach to cook our dinner. But alas, before we could enjoy a single taste, suddenly we heard the ship's horn blasting, and saw the Captain beckoning to us like a mad-man.

'Hurry aboard!' he cried as we hastened back. 'There is no time to lose! This place you have been walking over so innocently is not an island at all – it is a monstrous whale! It has been asleep upon the gently rocking sea-bed for so many years that seeds have drifted onto its back, rooted and grown into forests! But now with your tramping about and your fires, you have suddenly woken it. Look!'

We all turned back to see the 'island' heaving itself out of the waves: indeed, it really was a whale. As we watched, the gigantic creature flexed its muscles – and then it dived.

My friend, words cannot describe the horror of that moment. For the whale's bulk sent up a fountain of enough force to almost touch the very gates of Heaven; and the tidal wave that followed capsized our ship and tossed every man aboard straight into the foaming sea. I must tell you, with the deepest regret, that many of my companions were drowned. However, Allah (all praises be heaped upon Him) saved me by sending a wash-tub to my clutching hands. I drifted in this to a country where I found temporary work in the service of the king until I was able to buy a new passage home.

*The Second Voyage*
If you think that such an experience turned me into a land-lubber, you are quite wrong. Instead I was restless now for more adventure, and soon went voyaging again. This time we made landfall on a wild island of rocks and forests. While the crew set about fetching fresh water, I went off to explore at a bold pace, and walked some distance. Feeling tired, I lay down beneath a tree and promptly fell fast asleep. Some hours later I awoke – and was dismayed to discover that my absent-minded companions had sailed off without me!

Refusing to bewail my misfortune, I resolutely set out to ascertain whether any people lived here who might be of help. From the tree-top I perceived in the distance a great white

*Sindbad, stranded in the Valley of Diamonds, attaches himself to a joint
of meat and awaits rescue by a giant eagle.*
[British Library 12410.ff.16]

dome, and trekked for many hours through dense forest to reach it. It turned out to be a smooth, moon-coloured, spherical building, fashioned entirely without doors or windows. As I stared at it, the sky suddenly darkened: looking up, I saw the shadow of an approaching bird, a gigantic roc. It was then that I realised that this odd 'building' was, in fact, a roc's egg!

Luckily, the roc seemed not to see me, ant-small as I surely was to her enormous eyes. She roosted and slept on top of her egg, whilst I hatched out a bold plan of escape. Unfurling my turban, I formed it into a kind of rope, then used this to attach myself firmly to the roc's leg. She did not stir as I worked; but as soon as dawn painted the dark sky with skeins of gold and crimson, she spread her wings and took off. Far, far across the ocean she flew, whilst I dangled from her leg like a tag of thistledown.

At last we landed in an expanse of rocky desert punctuated only by barren mountains. Desperate for water, I climbed down to a snake-infested valley. At the bottom I found nothing to quench my thirst. Instead there was a dried up river-bed scattered with thousands – no, surely millions – of sparkling diamonds!

The next moment, something tumbled down the valley walls and hit me hard upon the shin. It was a huge lump of raw meat. As it rolled along, diamonds became stuck and embedded into the sticky red flesh. At once I remembered hearing of this famous trick, much used in remote lands by professional diamond hunters, and made haste to fill all my pockets and even my turban with diamonds. Then I picked up the meat and sat down to wait.

Before long, an enormous eagle swooped down and grabbed the meat in its beak, with me clinging tightly to it; so that as the eagle rose up with its meal, I was carried along. Beyond the mountains, the eagle was accosted by a band of the expected diamond hunters, who forced it to drop the meat (and myself) so that they could remove the diamonds within. As the eagle flew away, I displayed to these men the vast quantity of diamonds I had gathered, and offered to share them out. They treated me with the honour I had anticipated in return for this generosity, attending to all my needs, and even arranging for a safe passage to my home.

### The Third Voyage

My wanderlust by now had grown insatiable, so I did not remain at home for long. I joined a new ship, but before it could sail very far, we were invaded by pirates: hairy, ugly brutes, iron fisted and sharp toothed, half-way between dwarf-men and apes. They steered us to a remote island, dumped us all ashore, then sailed away in our own richly laden vessel.

Grateful to be alive, we wandered up the beach and sought shelter within a towering fort which stood nearby. There we all fell into exhausted sleep – and were woken at sunset by the noisy entrance of a

*Sindbad and his companions, abandoned on an island, take refuge in a deserted courtyard, where a colossal giant enters.*
[British Library K.T.C.19.b.10]

massive one-eyed giant. This monster locked the gates behind him, lit a fire and then suddenly seized one of my companions, threw him into a cauldron, boiled him alive, and gobbled him up!

We were trapped in this nightmare for many days, helplessly witnessing similar gruesome scenes many times over. At last, when all the fattest crew and passengers had been devoured, we scraggy survivors pulled ourselves together sufficiently to effect our escape. Firstly, as the giant slept, we blinded him by putting out his eye with a red-hot skewer; then, as he yelled with helpless pain, we climbed over the wall on a ladder built from his own benches, dragging them after us to serve as rafts once we reached the sea. Of course, the giant and his wife made pursuit, and the pair hurled boulders at us until most of my fellows were drowned. We survivors drifted on, until we found ourselves marooned on a coral island, whose shores were entwined by a gigantic sea-serpent. This monster proceeded to writhe and toss us about, before licking my friends up and swallowing them. However, I contrived to turn my raft into a lidded wooden box, which the sea-serpent spat out in disgust! After floating some way further in this, I was picked up at last by a cargo ship and in due course delivered safely to my home.

## The Fourth Voyage

My friend, you may call me foolhardy, but as soon as I could, I went travelling again. On this occasion I was shipwrecked onto an island ruled by a cannibal king, whose followers drugged and anointed my companions until their bellies swelled huge and their appetites grew insatiable. Then they were put out to graze, being fattened up for the pot. I myself managed to avoid this unsavoury process, though I almost starved to death as a result, and eventually slipped away to another, pleasanter country.

Here my enterprise and ingenuity amassed me such fame and wealth that I decided to settle down for a while; I even got married. My wife was a rich and amiable noblewoman and we lived in tranquil matrimonial bliss for some time.

But alas, the day came when my wife was stricken by illness and died. And then I discovered that this land had a horrific custom of

*Sindbad rests and refreshes himself after escaping from cannibals who have drugged and fattened-up his companions.*
[British Library 12410.ff.16]

always burying a bereaved spouse alive, alongside the body of the dead husband or wife. Thus I found myself incarcerated in a vast cavern, alongside not only my wife's corpse, but also countless other, more ancient skeletons! I survived there for some weeks in the most unspeakably macabre circumstances. Finally, by close observation I discovered that wild animals had been tunnelling into the burial pit in order to feed upon the plentiful supply of human carrion within: and this tunnel turned out to be my route of escape to freedom and eventual rescue.

## The Fifth Voyage

When I went travelling again, it was with an ignorant crew. Thus when we landed at another island where the roc birds nest, they did not recognise the great white dome-eggs for what they were. Before I could prevent it, they found one and began banging it about by way of crude examination: inevitably, it cracked open. The roc's revenge came as we sailed away that night. She and her flock flew after us, pelting us with boulders until our ship was smashed to smithereens.

Alone in the empty ocean, I was soon washed ashore to a lush and lovely island. I slept

*The Old Man of the Sea, who attaches himself to unsuspecting travellers, forcing them to carry him on their shoulders.*
[British Library Or. MS 4383, f.49r]

soundly there and ate heartily of its fruit, then set out to explore. Along a bubbling stream I was startled to come across a decrepit old man wearing a skirt made of palm fronds, and totally unable to talk. By way of signs and gestures, he indicated his desire to be carried across the water; and I, being charitable by nature, was happy to oblige. But no sooner was he mounted upon my back than I realised my mistake. For this was the infamous Old Man of the Sea, a kind of evil demon. He clung to me tightly with his beast-like legs, steadfastly refusing to let go, almost choking me with the vigour of his grip, kicking and beating me, forcing me to carry him further.

For many days and weeks, I was thus enslaved, with the old man pinioned to my back like a limpet. In the end, exhausted as I was, I managed to brew some wine from wild grapes and then tempted him to get so drunk that his muscles relaxed enough for me to throw him off and slay him with a rock. When at last a passing ship rescued me, its captain showered congratulations upon me, assuring me that I was the first person ever to escape alive from this foul creature.

*The Sixth Voyage*
So I arrived home and rested awhile; but the wanderlust still gnawed at my soul, so that I soon set off on yet another voyage. This one ended when we were wrecked onto a mountainous island whose beaches were covered in jewels, pearls, gem-stones, and morsels of preserved food. For a while we shared these sea-washed provisions; but one by one my fellows sickened and died until I was the only one left. In desperation, I built myself a driftwood raft, loaded it with precious litter from the beach, and set sail along a river that flowed straight into the heart of the mountain. For countless hours it swept me through the crushing darkness of narrow underground waterways, until at last I arrived at the lovely spice island of Serendib. The King that dwelt there received my offerings of jewels and gem-stones most graciously, and made me guest of honour at his court. At last, tiring of this endless fountain of exotic luxury, I persuaded him to arrange a ship to take me home; carrying on the king's behalf a great package of many wonderful gifts to my own Caliph.

*The Seventh Voyage*
I arrived home and, having presented the King's gifts, resolved to exchange adventure for a quiet

*Sindbad, captured as a slave, takes his master to see the elephant graveyard, and the great treasure of ivory.*
[British Library 12410.t.2]

life. However, after only a brief respite the Caliph commanded me to return to Serendib with some gifts from himself to the King: I was not permitted to refuse. The outward journey was uneventful, and my reception at Serendib joyful.

My luck turned, however, during the return journey, for our ship was captured and I was sold as a slave. The nabob who purchased me employed me as an elephant hunter, for he had a great lust for ivory. One day, whilst engaged in this hazardous pursuit, I was abducted by a great bull elephant that carried me away to what appeared to be an elephant graveyard. There, scattered amongst the outsize bones, I saw more ivory tusks than could ever be obtained in a dozen hunters' lifetimes! Naturally, this discovery made the hunting instantly superfluous. When I trudged back and reported it to my master, he was so delighted that he gave me immediate freedom.

Thus I returned home; resolving firmly that this would be my very last voyage. I had amassed many and marvellous riches on my various travels, and was received with great ceremony by the Caliph, who subsequently commissioned scribes to write down my extraordinary tale in letters of pure gold.

So now, grey haired and infinitely wiser, I am content to rest at home. But I will never cease to thank Allah (the compassionate, the merciful) for blessing me with a lifetime so full of adventure, and for granting me so many fortuitous escapes.

# Rama's Quest for Sita

Rama's quest for his wife Sita, kidnapped by Ravana the demon king of Lanka, is one of the oldest of Indian stories. It forms the core of the Sanskrit epic poem *Ramayana* attributed to the poet Valmiki, which tells the heroic deeds of Rama, prince of Ayodhya. Rama won the hand of Sita, princess of Mithila, but was exiled with his wife and brother Lakshmana to the forest (*see* fig. p.55) for 14 years through the plotting of his wicked stepmother. In the forest Sita was carried off by the demon Ravana, and Rama gathered an army of monkeys and bears to search for her. The monkey Hanuman jumped across the ocean to reach the island of Lanka where he believed her to have been taken (*see* fig. p.59). Rama and his allies attacked Lanka (*see* fig. p.61), killed Ravana, and rescued Sita. In order to prove her chastity, Sita entered fire, but was vindicated by the gods and restored to her husband. After the couple's triumphant return to Ayodhya, Rama's rule (*Ram-raj*) inaugurated a golden age for all mankind.

The story of the *Ramayana* falls naturally into two parts. The first part is a tale of intrigue at the court of Ayodhya, the capital of Koshala (roughly the present-day Indian state of Uttar Pradesh), of a sort that must have seemed natural among the petty kingdoms into which northern India was divided in the early first millennium BC. The first datable occurrence of the tale (to the middle of the first millennium BC) is to this first part only: Rama's exile to the forest is found among the *Jatakas* (previous birth stories of the Buddha), in which Rama as the Buddha-to-be exemplifies the virtues of filial obedience and renunciation. The second part of the epic, Sita's abduction and Rama's quest for her, is an altogether different, more magical, kind of tale, full of monstrous demons and talking animals. This is set vaguely in the south, which must originally have meant simply south of Koshala, but by historical times had been moved to the Deccan plateau, and to the island of Lanka or Ceylon, which became the stronghold of the demon king. This magical part of the tale, which also deals with Rama as a distraught lover and heroic warrior, was less suitable for expounding the Buddhist virtue of renunciation. We must suppose, however, that this part too was already known at that time and that the whole tale had been recited in bardic fashion for centuries.

Over the succeeding centuries the tale was much elaborated, becoming a huge poem of some 24,000 verses spread over seven large books. Into this epic but still human story was woven the perennial cosmic struggle between the good and evil forces in the universe. Ravana, himself semi-divine, had previously extracted a boon from the god Brahma that made him invincible to all the gods and other divine beings – he had not thought it necessary to obtain protection against mere men or animals. In order to destroy him, Vishnu the Preserver God had to be born as a man, and his only help could come from animals.

Valmiki's work is more than an epic; it is also considered the first poem, the *adi-kavya,* since Valmiki was moved by pity (*soka*) at the death of a love-bird to create the first verse (*sloka*) composed in the epic metre. Moved by this pity, he then went on to narrate the whole pitiful story of Rama and Sita in this newly created metre. Rama's laments for the vanished Sita as he wanders distraught through the forest form the poetic heart of the work, exemplifying in particular the sentiment of pity (*karuna-rasa*) which pervades the entire epic.

*Rama, Sita and Lakshmana begin their life of exile in the forest.*
[British Library Add. MS. 15296(1), f.70r]

It is difficult to exaggerate the influence of the story of Rama and of his quest for Sita on the whole of Indian culture. The two aspects of the epic, its poetic stature as well as its story, have moved India's writers over two millennia to emulate Valmiki. The story of Rama was constantly retold in poetic and dramatic versions by many of India's greatest Sanskrit writers in the first millennium AD: Bhasa, Kalidasa, Bhavabhuti, and their successors. In order to make the story more comprehensible to ordinary people ignorant of Sanskrit, versions were composed in Prakrits or early vernaculars. Nearly every major regional Indian language has its own classic version, of which those by Kampan in Tamil (twelfth century) and Tulsidas in Hindi (begun 1574) are the most famous. It is also one of the staples of later dramatic traditions, as in the Kathakali dance-dramas of the south, in puppet or shadow-puppet theatres, and in the annual *Ram-lilas*, or plays enacting Rama's deeds, of northern India. Bards still wander from village to village, retelling the story with the help of painted scrolls. Games of cards (*ganjifa*), chess sets, and so on, were devised using the basic oppositional plot.

Rama became identified as the seventh avatar (incarnation) of Vishnu, who in his divine role as Preserver of the World comes to earth to save it from periodic catastrophes, in this case from the ravages of the demonic Ravana. Sita was likewise identified with Vishnu's divine consort Lakshmi. Hindu temples were decorated with reliefs illustrating the story; the earliest major extant sequence of stone reliefs runs round the exterior walls of the Papanatha temple at Pattadakal in the Deccan, built in the early eighth century. Nearly a thousand years later, the story was still being told in this way, as on the walls of the Ramachandra temple at Vijayanagar, also in the Deccan, built in the early 16th century. This whole area

*Rama and Lakshmana guided by a sage set out to win Sita; an auspicious scene for the wall of a bridal chamber.* [British Library Add. Or. 3829].

with its forests and fantastic rocky outcrops had become identified with the monkey kingdom of Kishkindha. Such images in temples under royal patronage consciously evoked Rama, the ruler of Ayodhya in mankind's golden age, and were used as symbols of royal legitimacy.

Devotion to Rama became one of the most significant movements in later Hinduism, inaugurated in particular by Tulsidas's great poem *Ram-carit-manas* ('The Sacred-lake of Rama's Deeds'). Devotion could reach such heights that occasionally a raja would solemnly consecrate Rama ruler in his place and dedicate his kingdom to him, as was the case with Raja Jagat Singh (1637–72) of the Himalayan kingdom of Kulu, who ruled along with his successors as the god's vicegerents. It was Tulsidas and his immediate disciples in the early seventeenth century who began the tradition of *Ram-lila* ('Rama-play') during the Dasehra festival of northern India, a form of mass devotion in which the story of Rama and his quest for Sita is enacted by local communities, with boys taking the principal parts (*see* title-page). The climax of the festival commemorates the anniversary of the actual day when Rama finally slew Ravana. The action of a *Ram-lila* takes place not on a stage but throughout the town or village, so that given areas become Ayodhya or Lanka for the period, and the crowds act as citizens of these places, not just as spectators.

The story travelled in the first millennium AD to the various Hindu or Buddhist kingdoms of South-east Asia, brought with many other features of Indian culture by the sailors and merchants who regularly crossed the Bay of Bengal. Sometimes a distinct literary source can be traced, but other versions seem based on oral sources. In the ninth-tenth centuries was composed a poetical version in Old Javanese based partly on the eighth century Sanskrit version by the poet Bhatti. In Java also a great series of narrative reliefs of the Rama story was carved on the walls of the Hindu temples at Prambanam in the ninth century, and another at the eastern temple at Panataran in the fourteenth century. Although Java and Malaya later converted to Islam, the story is still told through the traditions of the drama, the dance and the shadow puppet-theatre, while the Malay version is one of the classics of that literature. In Bali which remained Hindu, and which preserved many traditions of Javanese Hindu culture, the story of Rama's quest is still central to Balinese life and is told in dramatic dancing and festivals, as well as by means of illustrated manuscripts and large painted hangings.

The kingdoms of mainland South-east Asia likewise were familiar with the story, and invoked Rama's kingship both in art and poetry as a model for their own kings' reigns. In the old Burmese capital of Pagan, Rama appears in the eleventh-twelfth centuries both as a former existence of the Buddha in a series of *jataka* tiles, and as a Hindu god. Another great series of narrative sculptures of the Battle of Lanka was created at the Khmer capital Angkor Wat in Cambodia in the twelfth century, while the old Thai capital Ayutthya founded in 1347 was modelled on Ayodhya. Even the conversion of the mainland to Buddhism did not bring an end to the story's influence: it has formed one of the main elements of Thai drama and shadow-puppet theatre since at least the fifteenth century, while the kings of Thailand themselves wrote several of the extant versions in the Thai language. New versions of the story were also written as poems and dramas in Burmese, Cambodian, and Laotian. In many of these versions Rama has become the Buddha-to-be and his Buddhist virtues are emphasised, but all of them change parts of the story significantly to reflect the different customs and cultures of their own countries.

Bali, Sugriva, Hanuman and the other great monkey chiefs are called the sons of various gods in the *Ramayana*. Bali is the son of Indra, the king of the gods, Sugriva of Surya the Sun-god, Hanuman of Anila the Wind-god and so on. At the time of the original composition of the epic, this was an obvious means of explaining the extraordinary prowess of these monkeys. When the epic was expanded to accommodate Rama as an avatar of Vishnu, come to earth as a man to destroy evil, the other gods too became incarnate in animal form as the monkey chiefs in order to help Rama in this great task of restoring good to the world. Of all the monkeys who had assisted Rama to recover Sita, it was the faithful and resourceful Hanuman, of immense strength and agility, who took most hold in the Indian popular imagination. He became the archetype of the faithful friend. In paintings he often stands alone with joined hands in front of the enthroned Rama and Sita, while Lakshmana stands behind waving a chowrie, thereby encapsulating the whole story as an icon. His wonderful exploits – his leap across the ocean, his bringing the magic herbs from the Himalayas to Lanka – endeared him to the common people in particular. He is often found alone in folk paintings, carrying the mountain of magic herbs, or wrestling with Ravana (fig. p. 62), or bearing Rama and Sita on his heart. In India, he remained wise, heroic and indeed saintly, but in South-east Asia where he is also the most popular character in the story, he became representative of all the freer aspects of life.

Rama and Sita – the two names are entwined together in Indian life. Their story of an ideal marriage, of Rama as the heroic husband who moves mountains to rescue his wife, and of Sita as his faithful partner, constant in adversity, has struck deep into the Indian psyche. Their conjoined names and presence impart blessings and fertility to every marriage (fig. opposite).

GOD is like the hidden fire in a fine-cut diamond, reflecting countless shafts of light. Within everything, beyond everything, the light flickers, sometimes catching the essence of Brahma the Creator; then again the great Preserver Vishnu, or Shiva the Destroyer. Yet still it is too vast, too dazzling, for human eyes to perceive.

The wheel of life turns. Good and evil struggle everlastingly: sometimes evil gains ascendancy. Then the light crystallises, takes form to restore the balance: then the gods walk upon Earth. Thus it was that, long ago, the light of Vishnu was born into Rama, the perfect man, and Sita the perfect woman.

* * *

Rama came walking through the forest, tearing his hair and groaning. He was like a demented man, broken under the crushing weight of despair, cursing all creation.

By and by he found he could walk no further, for his way was blocked by a vulture. Just as Rama was wounded in his soul, so this majestic bird suffered the gravest bodily affliction. For some while they regarded each other, man and bird, each wondering at the other's anguish; and then hoarsely the latter spoke.

'Greetings,' said he, 'I am Jatayu. Once I was king of all the vultures, but now I am dying from defeat in an ill-omened battle. And you?'

'I am Rama,' replied the other, 'rightful king of Ayodhya, but driven away into exile. I too feel that I am dying: of a broken heart and of shame, for my beloved wife has been snatched away from me.

The vulture peered at him more closely. 'Ah, so it is you,' he murmured. 'Though you may not have seen me, Rama, lately I have often sat by you in the forest, and wondered how so kingly a man was reduced to such pitiful circumstances. Your story must surely be a strange one. I beg you, tell it to me. Then, if I have strength left, I will try to help you – for perhaps I know what has become of your wife.'

'Have you seen her then? Jatayu, I beg you to tell me –'

'In good time, my friend. Be patient and explain yourself first.'

Rama sighed. 'It is not many years since my father, the old king of Ayodhya died,' he said, 'but even before he had drawn his last breath, I was ousted from my birthright. For I have a stepmother, an evil, scheming woman; and she forced my father to name my half-brother Bharata (totally against his will) as heir to the throne instead of me. Then she banished me into this forest for twice-seven years, precipitating my father's death.'

'But what of your wife?' enquired the vulture.

'Against my better judgement, she insisted on accompanying me. Even though I feared greatly for her safety in this wilderness, she would not forsake her marital duty to be always at my side. Oh, she has such virtue and faithfulness: I tell you, Jatayu, her whole nature is as flawless as her beauty, and without her company these years in exile would have been for me

*Sita has been captured by Ravana, who keeps her prisoner in the beautiful grove of ashoka trees in his palace in Lanka. Here he demands her love, while Hanuman hiding in a tree overhears.*
[British Library IO Skt. MS. 3621, f.3r]

pure torture. I did my utmost to protect her from every danger; and my brother Lakshmana who lives with us here, was ever as watchful as me. But, blinded by love, I allowed a whim of Sita's to distract us from our vigilance. This morning a gazelle bounded past our humble dwelling: its white coat shone like the moon, and Sita begged us to chase it, and bring it to her for a pet. As always, her wish was our command. We left her alone for only a brief time. But when we returned – without the gazelle, which had vanished as if by enchantment – Sita had vanished too.'

The wounded bird was struggling to talk: life was slowly draining from him.

'Hush, king, and listen,' he rasped. 'This morning I was dozing in my tree when I was woken by a dreadful screaming. Gazing across the sky, I saw the approach of a golden chariot. Within it sat the Rakshasa Ravana – that monster with twenty arms and ten heads; and clenched tightly against him was a marvellously radiant woman. It was her screams that had disturbed me. Naturally I rushed to her defence; and as I attacked Ravana with the full venom of my beak and talons, I heard him calling her by that very name.

'Sita,' he simpered, 'oh, my delicious Sita!' I was resolved to slay the Rakshasa and set free that innocent paragon of womanhood; but alas, his weaponry was far more potent than mine. So king, I suffered the humiliation of failure; and even worse, I was helpless to rescue your Sita from the prospect of endless suffering as foul Ravana's prisoner.'

'But which way did he go?' cried Rama, 'where has he taken her?'

'That I do not know,' whispered the vulture, 'but if you seek her, surely you will find her in the end. Now then, King, listen to this advice: do not be too proud to accept assistance from any other lowly being that may offer it; for all of creation is surely standing by to help you overcome this evil.'

With these words, the noble vulture died. As Rama stood, head bowed over its body, his brother Lakshmana came hurrying to him through the trees. Rama recounted all that he had heard. Then the brothers cremated Jatayu with the rites appropriate to one who has sacrificed himself to a higher cause, and prayed that his next life would reward him with enlightenment.

Rama's anguish was softened a little by some knowledge of Sita's fate: grim-faced, iron willed, he set off on the path to find her. He led Lakshmana through the mysterious ways of the forest, on and on, into the mountains. There on the summit of Rishyamukha, they met Sugriva, leader of the Great Monkeys, who persuaded Rama to seal a pact of brotherhood over the sacred fire. Then he told how he too had heard Sita's screams of terror, and seen her carried off by Ravana in his chariot, showing Rama his wife's veil and some jewels, which she had thrown down as she passed.

For a while Rama and Lakshmana stayed in the monkeys' realm. Their quest was delayed, for they had work to do there. Rama helped Sugriva to regain his authority; for he too had been usurped by unscrupulous members of his own family. After that task was fulfilled, the rains came, and Rama was forced to wait yet longer, his heart a pit of torment.

When the skies were dry again Sugriva sent out marshalls with instructions to call up every rank of the monkey army. From the north they came, from the south, the east and the west: from caves and forests, from mountains and deserts, from far and near, until millions of monkeys were assembled there. Sugriva divided them into four regiments, sending each one out to search one of the four quarters of the world: asking questions, scrutinising hidden places, watching, listening, always searching for Sita. In this way, a month passed; but Ravana's lair could not be found.

In the southern quarter, the search was led by the divine monkey Hanuman. Sired by the god of wind and hence imbued with his power, Hanuman was cunning, courageous and courteous. Rama observed this and placed faith in him: he gave Hanuman his ring, and begged him to present it to Sita as a token if ever he should find her. Hanuman guarded the ring carefully. He roamed with his troops far and further, until he came to that place where the land ends at the edge of the brooding ocean. There he met Sampati the vulture, who emerged from his cave to hear the monkeys' gossip. He was outraged to learn of the ignominious death of his brother Jatayu, and was eager to contribute to Rama's revenge.

'So,' he cried, 'this queen was abducted by Ravana, eh? Well, you have come to the right

*Rama and his monkey and bear allies begin the attack on Lanka.*
[British Library Add. MS. 15297(1), f.29r]

place, for I can tell you that this Rakshasa has his foul abode not far from here. It is just across the ocean, no more than one hundred leagues away, upon the lovely island of Lanka.'

When Hanuman heard these words, he drew deeply on his breath until his whole being was swollen with power; he ran up to the top of Mount Mahendra, and then he leaped. Like his father the wind, he sprang unfettered, across the ocean to Lanka in a single bound.

Now Hanuman shrank back into himself, until he was no larger than a cat. Night fell: he crept into the golden city, unremarked by any guard. Through the towering buildings he slunk, up the hill, across the walls, over the moat, and into Ravana's palace. On he went, passing like a shadow through store-rooms, throne-rooms and harems, always searching, never finding what he sought.

He passed out of the palace and through a forest, to a lonely *ashoka* grove. There at last he found Sita.

The evil Ravana was with her, begging her with blossomed words to yield to him; but the weeping queen would not. Then he began to bully her with black threats of starvation and torture if she would not become his wife: still she steadfastly refused. At last Ravana stormed out of her bower, flailing his twenty arms, gnashing the teeth in his ten loathsome heads, in a rage of unsatisfied lust.

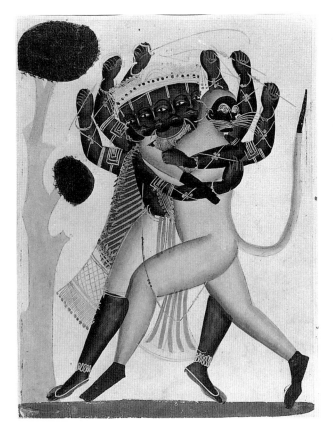

*Hanuman in single combat with Ravana.*
[British Library Add.Or. 891]

Good Hanuman was mindful of Sita's distress. When the Rakshasa had gone, he concealed himself in a tree, and began to chant softly like a song-bird, comforting Sita with songs in praise of Rama. Then he revealed himself; and to her joy, presented her with Rama's ring.

'My queen,' he said, 'now you have your husband's token, you know that you can trust me. Climb upon my back, I beg you, and let me carry you safely home, across the ocean, through all of India into the lofty mountains, where your own lord Rama is waiting to take you in his arms.'

But Sita's wisdom was deep as her sorrow. She said, 'I cannot come with you, good monkey. If I ride on your back, I might fall from it and thus return into Ravana's clutches. Besides, I have sworn that I shall touch no man or male creature except for Rama; and because he is my husband, the glory of my rescue and Ravana's destruction must go to Rama alone. So give him this jewel from me; and tell him, I wait for him to come.'

So Hanuman left her. Swiftly, he moved through the byways of Lanka, wreaking havoc as he went. Then he leaped back across the ocean, and with his army following behind, returned to the presence of Rama. When Rama heard that Sita was still alive – when he held the jewel she had sent in his own hand – then he embraced Hanuman as if the monkey were truly his brother.

Now that Ravana had been scented out, Rama was eager to launch an attack. Sugriva bowed to his request, calling together his four monkey armies and marching them down to Lanka. Behind them came a host of bears, led by their own monarch, Jambavan; for as Jatayu had prophesied, every being in the world wished to see Ravana's evil flushed out.

Soon they came to the ocean. There was no way to cross it. Rama prayed to it for three whole days, but it would not part its waters. Then he bombarded it with a rain of arrows until the whole world was darkened and the mountains shook. At last the ocean submitted to his will and allowed the building of a bridge.

For five days the monkeys and bears all laboured untiringly, carrying boulders and trees from the forest: thus the bridge was built. Then the army passed over it, across the ocean to Lanka, with Rama riding at the head.

Ravana's own malevolent soldiers were waiting there to meet them. Terrible was the battle that ensued, unfathomable the slaughter, unspeakable the wounds inflicted, innumerable the dead. And still it was not won.

At last, Ravana and Rama met each other face to face. They were like two blazing lions, with all passion unfurled.

Rama took up his great bow. One by one his arrows decapitated each of Ravana's ten monstrous heads. But at once, they all grew back.

Rama had one last arrow that was mightier than all the rest. Given him by the sage Agastya, its wings were moved by wind, its point was fashioned by fire and sunlight, its weight was greater than the mountains. Singing sacred mantras to sharpen its power, now Rama took this arrow and loosed it from his bow.

The arrow flew straight and true. It pierced the blackness of Ravana's heart, then flew back to Rama's quiver.

And Ravana died.

Then Sita was freed. She hurried to her king with love in her eyes; but at first he would not receive her, fearing that Ravana had violated her perfection. Then Sita's indignation gave her courage to match Rama's own: she commanded Lakshmana to build and light her own funeral pyre and stepped boldly into its flames. As the crowd watched, Agni the fire-god rose from the blaze, holding Sita aloft so that her inviolable purity shone out with the radiance of the morning sun. Then Rama understood that her love was as invincible as his own. He took her back to him, and together they went home to reclaim Ayodhya.

# Journey to the West

Although the modern version of the Chinese novel *Xiyouji*, 'Journey to the West', is attributed to the writer and minor official Wu Cheng'en (*c*.1500–82), antecedents are to be found in two works of the Song period (960–1279) and a Yuan period (1279–1368) music drama (*zaju*). The long history of storytelling in public, often with pictorial aids, has left no definitive evidence as to any origins in this genre. Outside China, one early Korean reader of the mid-fifteenth century, the *Pak t'ongsa onhae* is known. It is loosely based on the historical journeys of the Tang-period Buddhist monk Xuanzang (596–664, also known as Sanzang, or Tripitaka) who traversed the desert wastes across Chinese Central Asia to India, the home of Buddhism, to obtain unknown Buddhist scriptures (sutras) and bring them back to China.

The historical facts may be gleaned from such sources as a seventh-century biography of Xuanzang and *Xiyuji*, 'Record of Western Regions', a compilation which had been made by the year 646 from Xuanzang's notes and other accounts of India and neighbouring kingdoms by the monk Bianji, a member of Xuanzang's board of translators, set up to translate the Sanskrit Buddhist texts into Chinese. In 'Journey to the West', an imaginary account of the pilgrimage is elaborately expanded into a series of fictional, perilous encounters and battles with demons, monsters, animals and disguised deities from mythology, that are set up as obstacles to hinder the five pilgrims' progress towards their goal.

The novel opens with the story of the birth of Sun Wukong, Monkey, from a stone egg, his acquisition of magical powers and final incarceration beneath Wuxing shan, Mountain of the Five Elements, by the Buddha for his misdemeanours in Heaven. As a result of the ensuing Heavenly Council, the Buddha sends Guanyin, bodhisattva of compassion and mercy, to China to search out a scripture-pilgrim, Xuanzang. With Monkey's release (conditional on his accepting the opportunity to redeem himself), Xuanzang's other disciples are introduced: Pigsy (Zhu Bajie), Monk Sha (Sha Wujing, or Sha Heshang) and the dragon horse. Thus the setting is provided for the quest for the holy Buddhist scriptures which will save China and which will also lead the five pilgrims to atone for their previous sins.

Although the central character would, at first, seem to be Xuanzang, the overbearing personality of Monkey dominates the novel throughout. Taken as a whole, the quest for the sutras, explicitly stated in the narrative as being the source for China's salvation, can be interpreted as the need of the individual and humanity to overcome the trials and tribulations of life, in addition to the pursuit of personal salvation. The full range of wit and humour of the novel is manifested by means of Monkey's fully-rounded character which has endeared him to generations of readers. This device, however, also allows direct criticism of Chinese society and its religious and government institutions through the satirical comments he is permitted to make, and direct threats to authority in his railing against established figures. Pigsy embodies a certain brutishness and the insatiable desires of the senses. However, Monk Sha is less clearly drawn, although his nature has been defined by some commentators as one of innate sincerity, or

*The Sage Mother of Dongling, skilled in Daoist healing, rises on a cloud accompanied by a phoenix-like green bird, before a crowd of admirers.*

[British Library Add. MS 22689]

whole-heartedness. Thus, although by no means intruding on the narrative, a simple message containing the tenets of the Buddhist faith is worked into the account, together with an admixture of popular Daoist and Confucian philosophy.

Daoist beliefs are apparent, for example, in the appearance of spirits and deities from popular lore and mythology, and also in allusions to the search for immortality. This is admirably demonstrated in the famous episode of Monkey's stealing the peaches of immortality that take many thousands of years to ripen from the orchard of Xiwangmu, the Heavenly Queen Mother of the West, thereby ruining her banquet for the deities who reside in Heaven.

Monkeys in general, as well as Monkey from the novel, are frequently portrayed on Chinese ceramics and New Year prints holding a peach or vying to steal the fruits from peach trees – clearly an allusion to this event. (When a monkey and peach are shown together in the decorative arts of Japan and Korea, the association, while maintaining obvious connections with the Chinese theme, appears to lack any direct reference to the incident in the peach garden.) Also, in Monkey's acquisition of magical skills, such as transformations into a variety of shapes and leaping through the sky on his cloud-trapeze, he mimics the dexterity of Daoist adepts, immortals and deities (*see* fig. p.64).

A monkey character is central to all the versions of the 'Journey to the West' from its earliest appearance, and simian guardians to priests even occur in other early stories. However, to date, no satisfactory explanation as to why a monkey should be chosen as the hero has been provided.

Since its earliest appearance, it is clear that incidents from the story have appealed to all segments, high and low, of Chinese society. Apart from the Yuan period *zaju* dramatic performances, innumerable woodblock-printed editions of the tale were published, many illustrated, during the Ming (1368–1644) and Qing (1368–1644) periods (*see* figs pp.70 and 72). Similarly, characters and episodes from the story are found in abundance in many other popular art and craft forms up to the present. These include Peking opera, shadow puppets, papercuts, papier-mâché and plaster masks, sets of ornaments, playing cards, and children's toys made of plaster, dough and modern materials, comics and popular illustrated books, as well as cinematographic forms, such as animation. Although obviously lending themselves naturally to artistic treatment, there is a notable scarcity of representations of the countless adventures and encounters in the novel among the higher artistic forms such as painting, or even among the decorative arts, such as ceramics, which over the centuries have drawn widely on all manner of traditional and popular themes. For example, scenes from the Chinese stage are a major source for the decoration of blue-and-white porcelain, but neither episodes nor characters from the 'Journey to the West' are immediately in evidence.

Perhaps this reflects the fact that the vulgar nature of Monkey's escapades and his insolence in the face of authority were regarded as unworthy of serious consideration by the literati and scholar-amateur artists who dominated traditional cultural life, or even potters and other craftsmen who were dependent on the former group as their primary clientele. Indeed, while widely read by them, novels were frequently regarded as no more than what the term for the genre implies – *xiaoshuo* 'insignificant/petty words' – by the educated élite, who were trained to uphold the great Confucian tradition. With changing attitudes towards literature, twentieth century Chinese artists have turned their hands to producing paintings of this subject in traditional ink and colour techniques and modern styles.

As already noted, subject matter from the 'Journey to the West' appears rarely to have been used in the arts of Japan and Korea. One outstanding early Japanese woodblock example (dated 1383) of a scene taken from the story, however, is the frontispiece to the sutra *Mahāprajñāpāramitāsūtra* (the Japanese version of the Sanskrit given first: *Dai hannya haramitta-kyō*) 'Perfection of Wisdom'(*see* fig. p.68). Based on a Chinese exemplar, it shows Xuanzang receiving the holy scriptures from the Buddha.

While on their return journey to China, the pilgrims are confronted with yet another ordeal in order to bring the number of calamities to 81, the 'perfect' number in Chinese cosmological numerology. The magic gale on which they ride is withdrawn and the company fall to earth. Following this, the White Turtle, who is bearing them along the River that Flows to Heaven, overturns his load, including the sutras. At this point, historical fact and narrative fiction once more begin to coincide. Some scrolls were indeed lost when an elephant drowned on Xuanzang's actual return journey.

The exhausted travellers are treated to a rapturous reception in the capital, Chang'an (now Xi'an, Shaanxi province). Taizong, the emperor, makes provision for the installation of the newly acquired holy writings and for their translation. A board was, in fact, established for this purpose first at Chang'an and subsequently at Luoyang, the secondary capital. Originally, Xuanzang had held out great hopes for the building of a stone pagoda, more than 100 metres high, for the safe storage of the texts (traditional Chinese architecture employed timber as the main material). Unfortunately, he had to be content with the Greater Wild Goose Pagoda (Dayanta), the rebuilt structure of which stills stands today, to the south of Xi'an.

As the reward for the merit amassed in the perilous quest, Xuanzang is appointed to be the 'Buddha of Precocious Merit' and Monkey the 'Buddha Victorious in Strife'. Although washed of some of his past transgressions, Pigsy's only promotion is to that of 'Cleanser of the Altar'. His future task is to clear all Buddhist altars of offerings, his greed not yet having been extinguished. Finally, Monk Sha is given the rank of an arhat (one who is enlightened) and the horse that of a 'Senior Heavenly Dragon'.

*Xuanzang receiving the sutras from Buddha in Paradise.*
[British Library Or.64.b.16]

YOUR Imperial Majesty, Emperor of the Middle Kingdom, Son of Heaven: I kow-tow before you! With the greatest respect, I bring to you a most precious gift, carried to your palace all the way from the Western Paradise: five thousand and forty-eight scrolls of immeasurable holy wisdom. These are the true scriptures it is said that you have dreamed of, presented to you on behalf of the wise and compassionate Buddha. This is a gift truly beyond price, for the salvation of all mankind.

It has taken me all of fourteen long years to fetch it. In the course of my journey, I travelled over 108,000 leagues, traversing the highest, most inhospitable mountains, whose towering peaks seem to soar into the very offices of Heaven itself. During this journey, I have had travelling companions so strange, no poet could have imagined them. I have overcome no less than eighty-one terrifying, calamitous perils. Your majesty, I believe I may actually have died and then been reborn during that long, long journey: certainly I have experienced not just fear and suffering, but also great wonder and indescribable bliss. Now I humbly beg you to listen, for here is my story.

\* \* \*

I was born to a pious and simple family who gave me the name of Xuanzang. Being quiet, thoughtful and modest by inclination, on attaining manhood, I decided to take up practice amongst the ancient mysteries and rituals as a monk.

But then there came a fateful day when I received a visitation from the Goddess of Mercy, Guanyin. 'I come to you at the request of the holy Buddha,' she told me. 'We have chosen you to make the long journey westwards into Paradise. There you must obtain certain scrolls containing the Buddha's most sacred writings, and bring them back safely to share amongst your people.'

I have to confess it: at that moment my apprehension was very great. But only a demon could refuse Guanyin's gentle pleading and persuasion. And so, humbly and dutifully, I accepted the task allotted to me. It was in honour of this that the goddess bestowed upon me a new name; and so I became, and still am, Tripitaka-of-the-Big-Vehicle, Saviour of the Living, Saviour of the Souls of the dead.

When I set out, at Guanyin's command, under Guanyin's protection, I did not yet understand exactly where I was going to, or what my journey would involve. But I was lucky, for I was not expected to tread the long path alone. As I progressed, Guanyin sent me four courageous fellow travellers, each one of them a fair match for any danger we might meet.

One of these companions was an ill-shapen monster who took the name of Pigsy. He told me he had once been a spirit and dwelt in Heaven; but the Jade Emperor had expelled him on account of his drunkenness and illicit sex; his journey with me was his penance. Another was a creature called Sandy who wore a necklace of skulls around his neck, and had the power to change his own shape: for example, if we came to a river, he could transform himself into a

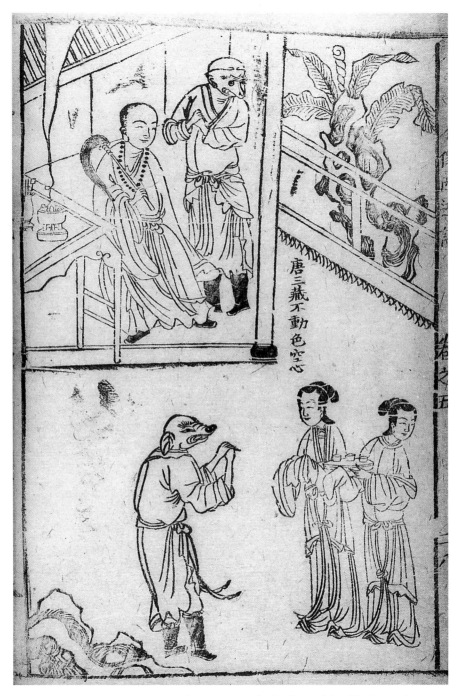

唐三藏不動色空心

*Pigsy succumbs to earthly desires by accepting food, observed by Monkey and Xuanzang.*

[British Library 15271.c.13]

boat, and carry us all across it. The third was the son of a dragon-king, who had committed the crime of rebellion against his own father. To atone for this, Heavenly officials compelled him to take the form of a white horse, and allow the rest of us to ride on his back.

As for the fourth companion: he was none other than the infamous Monkey, one time self-styled 'master of the universe', scourge of all the lords of Heaven. You may perhaps have heard the legend of his detestable exploits: how he challenged the rock of all authority, stole the Queen of Heaven's rare Peaches of Immortality, and almost replaced divine order with total anarchy. Indeed, the crimes of his past life were so numerous that the Buddha himself shut him up in a box buried far below the mountains, and left him confined there for five hundred years. Now, however, Monkey truly wished to repent for his sins and become a holy man like myself; thus he was freed and allowed to accompany and protect me on my journey. Nevertheless, he was still tainted by tricks and tantrums, with the courage and ferocity of a tiger!

We were an ill-assorted fellowship; yet together, the five of us, were invincible. Your Majesty, I shall not bore you with the long and tedious details of our journey. There were so many strange dwellings that we stopped by, so many curious beings whom we encountered and helped, so many unspeakable dangers and demonic creatures we had to outwit! On occasions we faced both slavery and wizardry. We rescued peasant children, minor kings and even hungry ghosts. We were the victors in a royal rain making competition. We visited exotic realms high in the swirling clouds, and others deep, deep under the waters. And so on, and so on, as our feet grew sore, our hair grey, and the years rolled by.

But at long last, we arrived at the Western Paradise. This country, Your Majesty, is like no other place I have ever seen. It is a jewelled garden, whose many shrubs bloom with gem-stones, whose grasses bend in the soft breeze like a tide of burnished silver. It is a land that teems with hermits, pilgrims and holy men, all smiling and swaying together in a great swathe of song. The towers that rise up there are all built of pure gold, for at the very heart of this Paradise stands the citadel of the holy Buddha.

Our arrival in this marvellous land had long been anticipated. The official who greeted us was himself an Immortal — one who had already attained the great secret of everlasting life. He wasted no time in directing us onward, towards the Holy Mountain, whose top was lost in mist, shimmering with the shifting colours of countless rainbows. And so, wearily, we walked on yet further, towards this mountain.

But now a wide river flowed across our way. We sought to cross it; and it was then that my whole being seemed to fall apart, and into a dream. For the boat which carried us over the water had no bottom to it; and when I looked down into it, I saw my own body in the water, gently drifting away down-stream! Then I understood at last, that this strange and perilous journey had taken place within my own soul, as well as through the efforts of my physical body; and my soul had reached its destination first. And so I watched my 'self' floating away, and felt the bliss of freedom and transcendent wisdom: I knew that the core of my being had already come home, to the Furthest Shore.

*Monkey with his iron staff and Pigsy with his muck rake engage the Bull Demon King.*

[British Library 15271.c.13]

Since that moment, my only wish has been to share such transcendent bliss with your Imperial Majesty — and thence with the whole world.

So in my dream state, mindless now of companionship or solitude, I drifted on. I went through meadows of flowers, where smiling creatures grazed: there were cranes and deer, even phoenixes. I floated up the Hill of Life, to the Temple of the Thunder Clap — and there I came into the blissful presence of the holy Buddha himself.

Now I was far beyond time. I do not know if I waited minutes or years before he spoke.

'There is greed in the Middle Kingdom,' said the Buddha. 'There is slaughter, lust and lying. There is desire for impossible things. I have wept for your people: I know how they suffer! But I shall give you my holy scriptures. Take them back with you. Tell your Emperor to read them to his people. Then they will learn the true way, the Middle Way. Then they shall be freed from the wheel of painful desires. And so, they will be saved.'

Now I looked and saw three great baskets standing at the Buddha's feet: each one was overflowing with paper scrolls. The Buddha said, 'Everything is here, all the wisdom in the world, inscribed on these 15,144 scrolls.' He paused, maybe for seconds, maybe for decades. I waited. He said, 'There are too many. I cannot let you have them all. The people of the Middle Kingdom are so excessively foolish and boisterous. Most of this would be beyond their understanding. Take these, instead.' He turned, he gestured. Behind him stood a row of chests and jewelled boxes, each one iridescent with beams of golden light. Servants came forward and opened them. They drew out piles of other scrolls and placed them into my outstretched arms.

'Open them!' said the Buddha. Now he was laughing. 'Read them! It is all there — everything you need to know.'

So I opened them, and looked. But these scrolls — they were all blank!

'You have offered me no payment,' the Buddha said, 'so in return, I have given you nothing.' Still, I waited. And then: 'But nothing is everything as you, Tripitaka, have already found. Such blank papers as these they are the true scriptures!'

I heard him and I understood, for had not my soul just completed its own long journey and found its way into the blissful nothingness of Paradise? Yet, my mission was to help all those others even such as your self, Your Majesty, who in your magnificence have not yet had time to even contemplate beginning such a journey. I could not bring nothing back to you.

So I waited even longer. 'Your gift,' the Buddha whispered at last. And he gave to me all these. There are five thousand and forty-eight scrolls here, each of them inscribed with the most profound and beautiful sacred writings.

I journeyed home through the clouds with them. I protected them through more calamities involving fierce storms and even fiercer demons.

Your Imperial Majesty: I have the greatest honour to present them to you now.

*Deluded sailors prepare a meal on a whale that they have mistaken for an island.*
[British Library Harley MS 4751, f.69]

# The Life of St Brendan

St Brendan (*c*.486–*c*.577) was an Irish monk who founded the monastery of Clonfert near Galway on the west coast of Ireland. During his lifetime he made at least two sea voyages as a form of pilgrimage, at once a physical trial and an opportunity to communicate with God in relative solitude. In the course of his voyages, Brendan visited hermits and isolated monastic communities at some distance from the Irish coast. However, his several monastic foundations represent his most lasting achievement as a churchman in Ireland. His memory is preserved to this day in many place names along the County Kerry coast, for example at Brandon Bay, Brandon Point, and Brandon Mountain.

To judge from the date of the earliest manuscripts, the Latin *Navigatio Sancti Brendani* (Voyage of St Brendan) in its surviving form was written no later than the end of the tenth century. The writer was probably Irish, but the provenance of the manuscripts suggests that he was living in Lotharingia (present-day Low Countries, Luxembourg, North-West Germany, Alsace and Lorraine). The work shows the clear influence of a form of Old Irish literature, *imrama*, accounts of fantastic sea voyages undertaken by secular heroes. Thus, for all its piety the *Navigatio* is very different in form and content from traditional saints' lives, with their emphasis on miracles, in life and posthumous. Indeed, the *Navigatio* relates strange events common also to non-Irish traditions, such as the sailors landing on a whale's back, thinking it to be an island, an incident that also occurs in the *Thousand and One Nights* (*see* The Seven Voyages of Sindbad the Sailor, pages 44–53); the same episode was also incorporated into medieval animal lore. The *Navigatio* was one of the most popular medieval texts, as is evidenced by the number of surviving manuscripts (at least 120) and by the number of translations into vernacular languages.

Brendan's quest takes the form of a journey to a promised land, the so-called Land of Promise of the Saints, which when reached affords Brendan and his followers a glimpse of the heavenly life promised to those who are saved. The voyage is in itself a test of physical and mental endurance, as the crew face frequent shortages of food and water and are tested by the extreme rigours of the weather. They are also attacked by monsters and aggressive islanders. Equally, however, they are assisted in their quest by various monks and hermits, who provide for their needs, by a whale, and by a dog that guides them to food.

The *Navigatio* has had considerable impact upon the history of exploration and cartography. 'St Brendan's Isle' appeared frequently on maps and charts until the end of the fifteenth century, including the famous *Mappa Mundi* in Hereford Cathedral. It appeared on occasions thereafter. It was generally located to the west of Ireland and often at a latitude sufficiently southerly to be confused with Madeira or the Canaries. Columbus, naturally, showed an interest in Brendan's Isle. Some seemingly fantastic features of the *Navigatio* do however have a possible basis in reality. The column of crystal could be an iceberg, surrounded by ice floes; the land of slag tips and forges, a volcanic island near Iceland; the thick mists, the fogs off the Grand Banks. Indeed, these possibilities and also the presence of factual details in the narrative so gripped the twentieth-century explorer Tim Severin that he constructed a curragh according to the description in the *Navigatio* and sailed it to Newfoundland in 1976–77. He thus succeeded not only in illustrating the skill and effectiveness of the seamanship of Brendan and his contemporaries, but also in demonstrating that Irish monks could have reached North America.

Brendan and his crew disembark on what they take to be an island but is in reality the back of a benevolent whale. Brendan's goal, the Land of Promise of the Saints is located to the north. In other maps its location is more southerly.

[From *Nova typis transacta navigatio Novi Orbis Indiae Occidentalis*. British Library G.7237]

IRELAND. *The Monastery of Clonfert.* The year of Our Lord 565. My quiet life of contemplation is no more: I am about to embark upon a perilous journey! This morning our saintly abbot, Father Brendan, called a small group of brethren together, announcing his intention to lead us across the ocean to the fabled Land of Promise of the Saints. The existence of this paradise has been revealed to him by his spiritual brother, Abbot Barinthus of Drumcullen; and Father Brendan declares that he desires nothing more of this world than to set eyes upon it for himself. I am one of fourteen fortunates chosen to accompany him. He warns us that the search will be long and arduous, and beset by spiritual conflict. I am most apprehensive, yet much honoured too.

Thus we are now in the process of preparing ourselves. For forty days we must each undertake a series of three-day fasts. After that cleansing is complete, we depart westwards towards the coast of Dingle to build ourselves a curragh, and thence to sail.

*I know not our location: we are somewhere lost upon the ocean.*
*Nor can I be sure of the date: I have lost all track of time.*

We find ourselves drifting helplessly, entirely yielded up into God's hands. Our simple curragh — fashioned from wood and ox-hide, waterproofed with fat — has proved surprisingly robust. However, it is somewhat cramped, for our numbers were unexpectedly swollen by the late arrival of three more brethren, who begged Father Brendan to take them aboard. He did so but openly expressed his misgivings that two of these may be surreptitious sinners who have freely chosen to sail towards some bitter judgement.

Such thoughts lie heavy on my heart just now, for the wind that blew us steadily for the first fifteen days has failed completely and we are totally becalmed. We have laid down our oars to conserve our strength: the food supplies are running low.

*Easter Day. 'The Island of Birds'.*

Already we have had several enlightening adventures; and now we are celebrating Our Lord's Resurrection in the most delightful of places. The calm of which I wrote in my last entry continued for all of forty days. Just as we began to fear death by starvation, God in his mercy drew us towards a high, rocky island that at first appeared impenetrable; but after circling it for three days, we finally entered a tiny harbour. From there a little dog of remarkable sagacity led us to a large hall, quite splendidly furnished and adorned with many ornaments. Though nobody was there to greet us, the tables were laid with a fine supper of white bread and fishes, and plentiful drink. Assured by our abbot that this was intended for us, we supped on it gladly, then lay down to sleep in the beds provided. We enjoyed this hospitality for three days, but all the while without any company. Then, much revived after our long ordeal at sea, we prepared to depart. That was the moment when our growing sense of complacency was shattered. For one of the three latecomer monks suddenly revealed that he had long been nurturing iniquity within his breast, and that he had thieved a silver necklace from our unseen hosts. Even as he confessed and repented, a shadowy demon-child seemed to leap darkly from his body. Father Brendan, in his infinite goodness, gave him immediate absolution; and then that unfortunate brother collapsed and died. Many of us saw his newly cleansed soul actually borne up to Heaven by a host of angels; but none the less, we were all shaken by this reminder that Lucifer wages an unceasing war against every man.

Thus chastened, we embarked again; but before the curragh was launched, we were approached by a godly young man – a steward of some kind – who offered us bread, water, and his blessing. We were glad to accept such generosity, and indeed were well sustained by it during our next voyage, which lasted many days.

By and by, a wind blew us towards a fertile island where grazed a flock of enormous sheep. At Father Brendan's behest, we selected one of these, with an unspotted lamb, and began to prepare them for the forthcoming Easter feast. As we worked the steward appeared again from nowhere, bearing more victuals, which he packed into our boat, explaining that we had not yet reached our resting place for the Easter vigil.

Accordingly, we rowed onward, landing at dusk upon a bare, rocky island, though our abbot declined to join us ashore. The next morning we gathered driftwood and proceeded to light several fires upon which to roast our meat. At this, the island suddenly began to heave and buck about like waves in a storm! Fortunately we all hastened back to the boat in safety; and as we rowed away Father Brendan explained that this apparent 'island' was really the vast monster fish, Jasconius.

Relieved at our escape, in time we came to this pleasant land. We are now camped beneath an enormous tree which is home to a myriad of pure white birds. These exquisite creatures have the gift of talking and singing with human speech. Moreover, their voices are blessed with such sweetness and purity as I have never heard before. At each of the seven canonical hours they burst out into a beautiful psalm in praise of Our Lord, all the while flapping their wings in unison. It transpires that once these birds were actually angels, but on some foolish whim they refused to condemn the sins of Lucifer, and hence were banished from Heaven and denied for ever more the true vision of God's glory. Despite this, they are the most delightful company, and I for one shall be truly sorry to bid them farewell. But that will not be until Pentecost. On that day, our steward has promised to return with further provisions for the next stage of our journey.

*Christmas Day. The Monastery of St Ailbe.*

After a further voyage of three months we were guided to this wonderfully peaceful island monastery. The abbot is a grave and dignified elder, whose eyes shine with the radiance of one in direct communion with his Maker. The brethren are equally dignified; for the past eighty years they have lived under a vow of silence, which is broken only by the regular singing of hymns. The bread which nourishes them arrives miraculously in their cellars each morning; moreover, the candles of their church are mysteriously lit each night by flaming arrows of spiritual fire like that of the Biblical 'burning bush'. Despite their venerable age, not one of these monks ever suffers any sickness or discomfort of mind or body: such a life of discipline clearly brings many blessings. What an uplifting place this is in which to celebrate Jesus Christ's wondrous birth.

*Date unknown. Place unknown.*

I am weak with enforced fasting: I fear we may be nearing starvation. And yet, like a tiny, frail feather resting in God's palm, I feel strangely at peace. Such sights I have seen! Such experiences I have witnessed . . .

We have all been intoxicated – on nothing stronger than pure spring water. We have found ourselves, trembling, in the midst of a battle between two gigantic sea-serpents (and afterwards feasted on the vanquished monster's delicious flesh!). We have floated in a haze of inactivity for months on end. We have endured an entire season of rain and hailstorms without respite. We have survived attack by a monstrous griffin. We have lost another of our latecomers (but joyfully this time) to a community of singing monks, who gave us in return a giant basket of luscious purple fruits. We have celebrated mass in the eerie, transparent centre of a crystal column whose top seemed to tower beyond the very sky. It seems that many years have already passed since last I inscribed this journal; for I clearly remember returning several times to the Island of Birds and on each occasion it was Easter. Likewise, we have often celebrated Christmas tide in the silent monastery of St Ailbe. Perchance, then, we are journeying through a spiral, and our final destination waits at its centre? Such thoughts cause my mind to dance and flicker, like sunlight on the endless waves . . .

But I must stop now and harness my strength, for our abbot predicts that even more gruelling adventures lie ahead.

*Date unknown. Before the gates of Hell.*

Am I awake, or is this some delirious nightmare? Some time ago, a strong wind began to blow us northward. In time, we came to a barren, stony island covered with ugly slag-heaps and smouldering forges. It was in this hell that evil-looking savages, as soon as they beheld us, began to hurl burning slag at our little boat. By rowing hard against the prevailing wind, we managed to escape this unprovoked attack, though many fire brands landed dangerously close to us in the frothing water. Our last view of that grim place was the whole island in flames, and the air filled with wailing and a dreadful, fetid stench.

The following day we came to a volcano with sheer black cliffs rising straight from the sea. As we sailed nervously past it, the last of the three latecomers suddenly fell from the coracle as if unseen hands were dragging him, and staggered, screaming, to the very shores of this infernal place. A swarm of demons, lurking in the shadows, then snatched him away into hideous torment. None of us could guess what shameful sin had caused Our Lord, in all his compassion, to condemn that lost brother to such a fate.

Mortified, we drifted on under heavy, doom-laden skies for another seven days. Then we came to a lonely rock to which a wretched man could be seen clinging, horribly battered by the waves and gale like a sodden piece of cloth. We sailed close enough to talk with him; and Father Brendan urged him to tell us who he was and what was the cause of his suffering. His answer made our blood run cold. 'I am Judas Iscariot,' said he. Then he explained that his present state was in fact a brief but very welcome respite from his true punishment, which consists of burning continuously like a lump of lead in a crucible. At nightfall he was destined to return to that endless torture; and though Father Brendan, moved by pity for a fellow human, managed to delay the demons when they came for him, it was not for long.

As I write, the long night is fading. The rock is empty: Judas Iscariot has gone. I feel strangely purged. And still we are drawn onwards, across the boundless ocean.


*Easter. The year of Our Lord 572. The Island of Birds.*


We are celebrating the Resurrection in this lovely island yet again: I believe this will be the last time. When we departed from the dark waters of Hell, I had no idea that it was already full seven years since we had set out from Ireland; but thus Father Brendan assures us. Between Hell and here, we have chanced upon a hermit whose sanctity greatly refreshed our souls after that last horrific vision. His name is Paul, and he inhabits a small cave upon the summit of a very lonely island. He is, he says, all of 140 years old; and though once a sea-otter used to bring him regular offerings of fish, his only nourishment for the last thirty years has been water. We were all greatly honoured to receive his blessing.


*It is perpetual summer. The year of Our Lord 572. The Land of Promise of the Saints.*


We are here! My heart flows over with such happiness that no words can adequately express. This paradise lies no more than 40 days' voyage from the islands where we spent each of the last seven Easters! Had we but known it . . . And yet, God moves the affairs of men to his own purpose, and I see that without first testing our endurance and our faith, we could never have gained entry to this place. For this island cannot be perceived by the unvirtuous: it lies perpetually shrouded by impenetrable mists that part only for the spiritually pure. However, once grace is achieved, it is possible to sail through with ease. Thus we emerged at last into a golden light glowing upon an idyllic country, thickly wooded with bountiful apple trees. We have been resting here now for forty days, tirelessly eating the promised fruit that is marvellously sweet, and marvelling at such vistas as would make the green hills of Ireland seem deserts by comparison. Now we are seated by a great river that seems to divide this land in two. A young man was waiting for us by its banks: he greeted each of us joyfully by name, but under no circumstances would he permit any of us to cross.

I am no longer troubled by yearnings, and I have lost all fear. I can glimpse the shining country that lies beyond this river and know for certain that I will reach it when my time comes. Father Brendan prophesies we will all return home to Ireland first: so be it. I am content, and my soul has found perfect peace: nothing has been in vain.

*Miniature from the opening leaf of the* Estoire del Saint Graal; *the author prostrate before the Grail with the hand of God above. The illuminated border contains a grotesque monster and an angel carrying an organ.*
[British Library Royal MS 14.E.iii, f.3 (detail)]

# The Quest for the Holy Grail

The Holy Grail appears first in a written text in Chrétien de Troyes's Old French verse romance the *Conte del Graal* ('Story of the Grail'), or *Perceval*, of *c*.1180. During the next fifty years several works, both in verse and prose, were composed, although the story varies from one work to another. Indeed, the particular hero also varies, even though most of the principal characters appear in the majority of the texts. One reason for this variety is that the Grail legend predates the *Conte*: Chrétien himself refers to a book that he had been given. Oral versions probably existed as well.

The origin of the Grail and its properties can be convincingly traced to the Irish myths of an earlier period in which heroes visited magic palaces of the gods or of former kings and were lavishly treated by their hosts, some of whom possessed a magic vessel. The major motifs of the legend crossed from Ireland, via Wales, to Brittany whence they spread to the rest of France and the Continent. During this process, the original meaning of the Celtic myths and the significance of their symbols were obscured or lost, and on occasions misunderstood, while at the same time the legend became imbued with contemporary ideas. The Grail legend is indissolubly linked to the story of King Arthur and his knights, for whom the search for the Holy Grail was the ultimate quest. The Arthurian legends followed the same route of transmission as those of the Grail. The medieval Grail romances were translated from Old French into the other major European languages. Two works in languages other than French stand out as being more than translations. One is Wolfram von Eschenbach's *Parzifal* (early thirteenth century), the other Sir Thomas Malory's *Morte Darthur* (late fifteenth century). Both authors interpret the quest in terms that amount to a personal vision of its moral and spiritual significance.

Just as there was no single version of the Grail legend in the Middle Ages, so there is no single explanation of what the Grail was. It is depicted in various physical forms: dish, chalice, ciborium and in the German *Parzifal*, it is a stone. Its origin can be convincingly traced to the magic vessels – dishes and cauldrons – of Celtic mythology which satisfied the tastes and appetites of all who ate or drank from them. In the Grail stories, the vessel appears in a similar setting of castle or palace and it retains magic properties although their nature has changed significantly. Once a horn of plenty, it has now acquired the power to heal grievous wounds and in time this power becomes symbolic of a spiritual process. The form of the vessel also changes and it acquires a Christian history. Chrétien envisaged a deep dish, although illustrators depicted it as a ciborium or as a chalice. This last representation stems from the Grail's identification with the cup of the Last Supper, in which, according to some versions, Joseph of Arimathea is said to have preserved some of the blood of the Crucified Christ. In other texts it is identified with the dish of the Last Supper and its depiction varies accordingly. A number of actual relics have been claimed as the Holy Grail, or as the cup of the Last Supper: for example, a glass chalice, known as the Antioch cup; the Holy Chalice of Valencia Cathedral; and, more recently, an obscure Roman onyx jar, found in Shropshire in 1920.

The medieval Grail texts fall into two categories. One group tells of the quest itself, the search by Arthur's knights for the magic vessel that has the power to heal a wounded king, reviving his barren kingdom and to win the successful knight a spiritual reward. This last aspect culminates in the anonymous French prose romance the *Queste del Saint Graal* (Quest for the Holy Grail) in which only the perfect knight, valorous and morally pure, can achieve the ultimate quest, having overcome all manner of trials and tests in the process. Galahad alone attains the Grail and the status of perfect knight, although others do see, or glimpse, the Grail. The second group of texts tells of the vessel's early history, from the Crucifixion to the time of Merlin and of its passage from the Holy Land to Avalon.

With the passing of the Middle Ages, the Grail disappears until the nineteenth century when medieval history and legend awoke the interest of writers, such as Scott and Tennyson, of the Pre-Raphaelites and other artists, and of composers, notably Richard Wagner. With Tennyson's *The Holy Grail* and Wagner's *Parsifal*, the Grail becomes yet more clearly identified with the cup of the Last Supper and is invariably represented pictorially as a chalice. Interest in the Grail as a mysterious object of search and also as the source of some ultimate mystical experience has persisted into the present century in the novels of Charles Williams, John Cowper Powys and C. S. Lewis.

IN ancient times a saintly man named Joseph of Arimathea came from distant lands, carrying the message of Christ's truth and love to lighten the ignorance that once shadowed the isles of Britain. And he also brought a marvellous dish, from which it is said that Our Lord ate the paschal lamb at the Last Supper, sharing it with his Apostles; moreover, this same dish contained some drops of Christ's own blood, shed when a lance pierced his side as he hung upon the cross. This dish was the Holy Grail.

Left: *Miniature from the opening leaf of the* Estoire del Saint Graal; *Christ appears to the author and hands him a book containing the Grail story. The Grail is visible on the altar to the left.*
[British Library Royal MS 14.E.iii, f.3 (detail)]
Right: *Josephe, Bishop of Sarras and son of Joseph of Arimathea, promises to entrust the Holy Grail when he dies to Alain, the twelfth son of Bron. Josephe and his companions sit at the table of the Grail, while Alain kneels in prayer.*
[British Library Add MS 10292, f.65]

For many centuries the Grail lay quietly hidden within the lost Castle of Corbenic, guarded by Joseph's own descendants, the noble Fisher Kings. But a time came when affliction and foul enchantments began to spread across the realm. Then pious men and women remembered the Grail and urged that it be sought out; for they hoped that its sacred mysteries might heal where human efforts had failed.

Now, at that time, King Arthur had his court at Camelot, with the allegiance of one-hundred-and-fifty brave and noble knights, the like of which the world has never known. And when talk turned to questing for the Holy Grail, each one of these fine men offered up his life to travel forth and search for it.

Arthur's people wept freely to see their noble guardians leave for the wide and unknown world, and none was as sad as the King himself, for he guessed that none would return quickly, and that many would die along the way.

So the knights set out. Each one met with strange and marvellous adventures which, alas, are too many to relate. But let us follow closely the fortunes of two: bold Sir Lancelot and his son Galahad the fair. For from what befell them, we may learn something of the Grail's mysteries, and perhaps also help those who hope to tread their own long path towards grace.

*   *   *

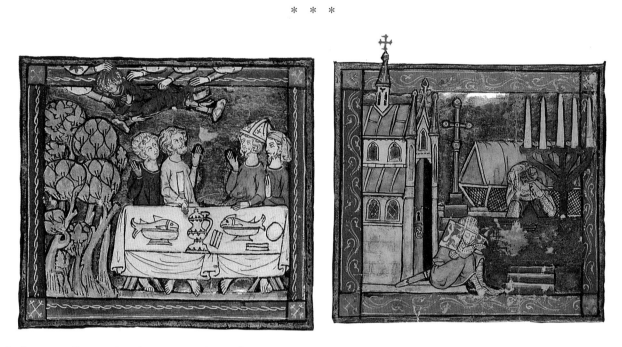

Left: *Seven flaming hands appear and cast fire upon Moys, carrying him away when he presumes to sit at the table of the Grail. Josephe, the Bishop of Sarras and son of Joseph of Arimathea, had warned him that the spare place would remain vacant until taken by one who was worthy. The seat is the 'Siege Perilous', symbolic of the place occupied by Christ at the Last Supper.*
[British Library Royal MS 14.E.iii, f.76v]
Right: *A wounded knight, carried on a litter, awaits the appearance of the Grail, which will cure him. Lancelot, meanwhile, is incapable of reacting because of the weight of his sins.*
[British Library Royal MS 14.E.iii, f.99]

When Sir Lancelot set out upon the quest, he left a broken heart behind: it belonged to the Queen herself, the lovely Guinevere, who to her shame long had valued that knight's furtive love above that of King Arthur her lawful husband. As Lancelot travelled, the honeyed darkness of the Queen's memory went with him. At first he carried it willingly and carefully, like some precious treasure; but as his journey progressed, it slowly seemed to tarnish, until its true nature was revealed to him in all its sin, and it became an intolerable burden.

Chastened by this revelation, one night Lancelot rode without stopping to rest as darkness fell, continuing through a thick forest until he came to a ruined chapel. Entrance to this place was barred by an impenetrable iron grille; and beyond it he saw an altar which was very richly adorned. He was weary by now and lay down beside this place. But sleep would not come to him: instead he was visited by a waking dream whose marvels deeply unsettled his soul.

In this vision he found himself paralysed, completely unable to move. And as he lay there helplessly, a sickly knight was carried by litter into the chapel. A silver candlestick and a silver table floated as if by themselves straight after him; and upon the table Lancelot believed he saw the Holy Grail.

The sickly knight fell to the ground and prayed, then kissed the Grail table – and all at once was healed. He armed himself, taking Lancelot's own sword and helmet and riding away on his horse. Finally, the sacred objects vanished.

*Galahad arrives at an abbey where he is greeted by two other knights of the Round Table, King Baudemagus and Ywein.*
[British Library Royal MS 14.E.iii, f.93v]

At this, Lancelot's limbs were suddenly freed: trembling, he rose to his feet. And from the darkness, a voice seemed to cry to him:

*Go! Take your foul presence away from this holy place.*

So, unarmed and on foot like a beggar, Lancelot slunk away through the wilderness until he came to a hermitage. The hermit who dwelt there was a true man of God. He celebrated mass with Lancelot, then offered to hear his confession. Humbly the bold knight bared his soul, admitting openly to his long adultery with the Queen, and confessing frankly that he owed all his wealth, status and glory only to her favours. The hermit replied severely on the evils of fornication, and on how such acts had betrayed and wasted the generous divine gifts bestowed upon Lancelot at his birth. Lancelot, searching deep within his conscience, now began to deplore this whole affair.

In time the hermit found him a new horse and fresh arms and Lancelot travelled on, haunted by the realisation that his supposed love for the Queen in truth had been a trap laid for him by the Devil. To atone for his past weakness, he resolved not only to renounce all acts and desires of the flesh, but also constantly to wear a hair-shirt, to foresake all tastes of meat and wine, and to attend mass daily if he could.

In this manner he continued his journey, stopping here and there at castles and hermitages, fighting in knightly battles in which victory strangely eluded him, taking joy in his new life of asceticism, confessing and listening to every saintly person he might meet. His final remnant of pride was shed when a holy woman explained that his previous worldly status was worth nothing in the Lord's eyes.

One day, on reaching a river that he could not cross, he waited and prayed with new found patience for Christ's help. Presently he saw a boat drifting into the shore, which he boarded. For many months he sailed in this mysterious vessel, out on the open sea, and gradually his soul was lightened by the sweet scents of paradise, and nourished by spiritual food. Many adventures happened in that time, but of all these, he treasured most an unexpected meeting with his beloved son, Sir Galahad, of whom we shall presently learn. Many tears were wept on both sides when they were called upon to part, for they were not destined to meet again in this world.

At last, in solitude, Lancelot found himself carried to a shore where the sea washed up to the Castle of Corbenic — that very place he had feared he would never find. Passing through a guard of fawning lions, he found himself before a locked door. From beyond it came the most exquisite strains of music; and when his prayers were answered and the door flew open, he gazed into a room flooded with golden light. Within its centre, he glimpsed for a second time, a vision of the Holy Grail. It seemed now to be tantalisingly close, for repentance had lightened his soul with some small measure of grace. But as he struggled to reach it, the dark weight of his past sins welled up against his longing: so that he was struck down by a fireball, and thrust out from the chamber by invisible angels' hands.

The good people who lived in that castle took him, lifeless as he seemed, and nursed him for all of four-and-twenty days, each day being payment for a year he had previously spent in the service of the Devil. After this, his body was cured. But realising that he would not be permitted to carry his burden any closer to Christ's vessel, wretchedly he resolved to end his part in the quest. Thus he returned home to Arthur's court, where his salutary story was told beside those of other, lesser knights, who had achieved nothing through their own adventures except varying measures of shame.

* * *

Such was the fate of a knight whose fame was tainted by worldly corruption. But his son, Sir Galahad met a different end, for his own soul was near perfection: never had he lain with a woman, nor had he ever desired to do so, even in his darkest dreams.

The histories tell how this Galahad was born of the Fisher King's own daughter, though begotten in a fog of sin by the fallen Lancelot, who was tricked to believe that the woman he lay with was Guinevere, his illicit lover. Fair Galahad's knightly skill and strength was gifted by his father; but his eyes shone with all the purity of his saintly mother's line.

He was raised in a nunnery, and sent to Camelot when he came of age, where at once King Arthur and his court recognised him as the Perfect Knight. For he alone could sit unharmed in Camelot's mysterious Seat of Danger; he alone had strength to draw the sword from the marble river stone; he alone was strong enough to bear the shield reserved *'for the totally virtuous'*. With these miraculous signs, good Sir Galahad rode out with the rest of the companions, then parted from them to wander far and wide. Many and marvellous were his deeds upon the way; but through each one he avoided any pride, covetousness or thought of lust; always vanquishing evil, protecting the weak, and putting villains to rout.

It happened that Galahad rested one night at a hermitage; from which he was summonsed from his bed by a gentle maiden who urged him to ride hastily with her towards the sea where a beautiful ship awaited him. On board he was welcomed by good Sir Bors and Sir Perceval, for these two chaste fellow knights of King Arthur's court were destined to be Galahad's companions in the quest. Their happiness was great at meeting each other, and their conversation was long, for all had much to tell of the dangers each had overcome, and of how they had successfully repelled temptations when the Devil tried to turn them from their way.

Then the maiden revealed herself to be Perceval's own lost sister, and when the ship arrived at a lonely islet, she led them across some rocks to another vessel, even more magnificent than the last. An inscription on its side allowed entry only to *'the perfectly pure whose faith in Christ is absolute'*. All four bowed boldly before it and stepped on board, where they found a sumptuous bed on which lay the Sword of the Strange Belt, inscribed for *'the most exceptionally excellent person'*. Sir Galahad claimed it as his.

Returning to their own ship they sailed on to the mainland, then rode further through more remarkable adventures and visions. In time they parted, and Galahad came alone to find his loving father Lancelot on the river boat, as was related above. Then he journeyed on for five more years, bringing comfort to the sick and purging the wicked of their sin as he passed.

At last he came again into the company of Perceval and Bors. Together these three were the paragon of chastity and gallantry; together, in joy, they reached the Castle of Corbenic and greeted Pelles, the last Fisher King. And at that moment a strange storm blew up with the breath of flames at its heart; and a voice cried:

> *'Let all sinners depart!*
> *For now the true knights shall taste the food of heaven*
> *at Christ's own table.'*

So the Fisher King's hall was emptied except for Galahad, Perceval and Bors. Next there entered nine stranger knights drawn from distant places: now there were twelve, in echo of the Lord's Apostles.

These twelve were seated round a table: they waited and watched. Soon there descended from Heaven, upon a throne borne by four angels, Josephus, the first Christian bishop. Turning, they saw him carried before a silver table, and on that table – there stood the Holy Grail. Then the angels brought candles, a scarlet cloth, and a lance from which the Lord's blood dripped softly into the sacred dish.

Bishop Josephus consecrated the mass; and a child-like figure fell from above to enter the bread, which in turn transformed itself into the vision of a human form. As Josephus embraced

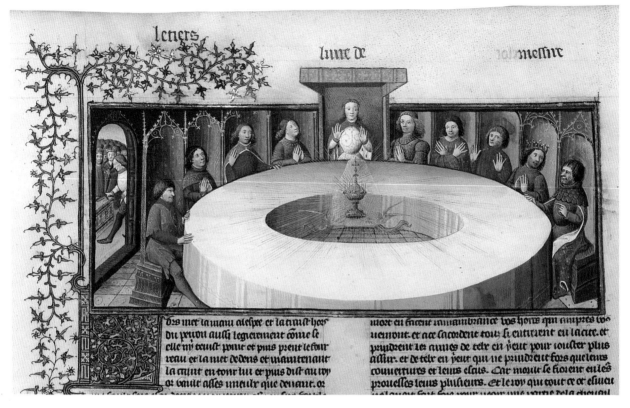

*Galahad, sitting in the Siege Perilous, the Knights of the Round Table and King Arthur (second from right) contemplate the Holy Grail. The mysterious vessel emits golden rays, clearly representing divine grace. Through the open door a preceding episode in the* Queste *is glimpsed when Galahad drew the sword from the stone found floating in the river, thus confirming him as supreme among knights.*
[Paris, Bibliothèque Nationale MS Fr. 120, f.524v]

Galahad, and he in turn the others, a man appeared from within the Grail. Unclothed, He was, and bleeding where nails had pierced His hands and feet and the lance had cut His side.

'My faithful sons,' said He, 'you who have striven so diligently for the spiritual life whilst still bound within the flesh, you have won the right to see deep into my mysteries, and to taste the precious food you long have craved through your sufferings.'

So he took the Grail to Galahad, and thence to each one; and as they tasted from it, their hearts overflowed at its delectable sweetness.

'And yet,' said He, 'even as you have found your hearts' desire, you must hasten to carry it away. For excepting yourselves, the people that dwell in this land are too sinful and weak to be trusted any longer with keeping it safe.'

Thus it was, after He blessed them and vanished, after the nine stranger knights had all dispersed, Galahad, Bors and Perceval set out yet again, sailing across the ocean to the far city of

Sarras. Here the three endured further trials. But in time Galahad was made the beloved yet humble king of that land; and his last earthly task was to build over the Holy Grail a magnificent ark of gold and precious stones. Then, having shown him once more the awesome glory of its mysteries, Our Lord granted his wish, and permitted him to pass away to heaven.

Perceval died too, a short time later, equally at peace for he had entered holy orders. So it was left to good Sir Bors to return alone to Camelot, and to tell how the Quest for the Holy Grail had come to its fulfilment.

# Notes on the works illustrated

*Notes on the works illustrated*

## JASON AND THE QUEST FOR THE GOLDEN FLEECE

*[p.9]* Jason rows out from Colchis.
[British Library Royal MS 20 D.i, f.33v]
*Histoire universelle*. Naples, mid fourteenth century.
A longer, revised version of the thirteenth-century French world chronicle, the *Histoire universelle*, appears to have been produced in the following century. This revision did not achieve the popularity of the original text and is now preserved in only a few manuscripts. Its earliest representative is a very fine, richly illustrated product of some of the best book producers of fourteenth-century Naples. Its destined owner was one of the ruling Angevin family at whose court a keen interest was shown in French romances. Subsequently the volume passed into the libraries of Charles V and his brother Jean de Berry.

*[p.10]* Pelias persuades Jason to build the Argo.
[British Library Add. MS 15268, f.105v]
From the *Histoire universelle*. Acre, c.1285.
This volume is one of three early manuscripts of the *Histoire* that have been attributed to book producers working in the coastal city of Acre which was then controlled by the crusaders from the West. The artists responsible for the miniatures reveal the influence of both the native artistic styles of their western patrons and the sophisticated art of Byzantium which the crusaders had also seized in 1204.

*[p.12]* Jason fighting the dragon which guards the golden ram.
[British Library Add. MS 10290, f.106v]
From the *Historie van Jason*. North Netherlands (Haarlem?), c.1475–1480.
In around 1460 Raoul Lefèvre composed a French prose account of the life of Jason which he dedicated to Philip the Good, Duke of Burgundy. This *Histoire de Jason*, which proved to be a popular work, was revised by the author in 1467 and printed in around 1476–78. An English translation by William Caxton was printed at Westminster in around 1477. The Middle Dutch translation was first printed by Jacob Bellaert at Haarlem in 1484–85 using the present manuscript as his model.
In the preface to Lefèvre's text Jason appears to the author and appeals to him to retell his story to the Duke and excuse his desertion of Medea. This text is therefore very closely tied to moral debate over Jason's worthiness to be the patron of the Burgundian chivalric Order of the Golden Fleece.

*[p.13]* Jason escapes with the golden ram.
[British Library Stowe MS 54, f.38v]
From *Histoire universelle*. Paris, early fifteenth century.
Soon after it came to Paris, the Neapolitan manuscript [p.9] spawned two further illustrated copies of the later version of the *Histoire universelle*. One which was sold to Jean de Berry in 1402 (now Paris, Bibl. Nat., MS fr. 301) contains very literal copies by Parisian miniaturists of the illustrations of the older manuscript. In the other the miniatures freely elaborate upon their models, while at the same time repeating the very unusual four full-page miniatures to illustrate the story of Troy. All the illustrations in this second manuscript, including those reproduced above, have been attributed to a Netherlandish artist working in Paris around the beginning of the fifteenth century.

*[p.14]* Medea appears in a magic chariot pulled by fire-breathing dragons.
[British Library Royal MS 20 D.i, f.37v]
From *Histoire universelle*. Naples, mid fourteenth century, as p.9 above.

## THE HOMECOMING OF ODYSSEUS

*[p.17]* The fall of Troy.
[British Library Stowe MS 54, f.203]
From *Histoire universelle*. Paris, early fifteenth century, as p.13 above.

*[p.19]* Penelope, the patient wife of Odysseus.
[British Library Royal MS 16 G.v, f.45v]
From Giovanni Boccaccio, *De claris mulieribus*, in an anonymous French translation. Rouen, c.1440.
In his treatise *De claris mulieribus* the Italian scholar and author Giovanni Boccaccio illustrates the theme of the vicissitudes of Fortune by retelling a long series of stories about famous women. Like his treatise 'On the Fall of Famous Men', Boccaccio's

work on famous women very quickly achieved great popularity and influence throughout late medieval Europe. In France an anonymous French translation completed in 1401 was copied and profusely illustrated in luxury volumes intended for many of the most wealthy and powerful nobles at the court in Paris.

Like the Talbot miscellany [p.36], this manuscript of the French translation of Boccaccio was produced at Rouen. It was probably produced for another English noble, possibly one of those who, like Talbot, formed part of the army still occupying that part of France.

*[p.20]* Odysseus and his men burn out the drunken Polyphemus' single eye.

[British Library C.77.i.9, opp. p.113]

From *Homer, His Odysses translated, adorned with sculpture and illustrated with annotations, by James Ogilby, Master of His Majesties Revells in the Kingdom of Ireland*. London: Thomas Roycroft, 1665.

In 1665 the former dancing master James Ogilby (1600–1676) had published his new translation of Homer's *Odyssey*. As in the case of his earlier translation of Homer's *Iliad* (1660), the text was spaciously laid out in royal folio sheets and generously illustrated with full-page engravings opposite the opening of each of its twenty-four books. The elaborate frontispiece was, like the engraving of Polyphemus at the beginning of Book 9, based on an original design by Abraham van Diepenbeeck, a pupil of Rubens. A further large engraving after Sir Peter Lely depicted the work's dedicatee James Duke of Ormond.

## THE TALE OF CUPID AND PSYCHE

*[p.24]* Illuminated page from the first printed edition of *The Golden Ass*.

[British Library G.8997]

From [The Works of Apuleius, including The Metamorphoses]. Rome [Swenheym & Pannartz], 1469.

This is the first printed edition of Apuleius' works. His stories appealed greatly to Renaissance audiences, and this was one of the earliest books to be produced after printing was introduced into Italy in 1465. This copy contains two pages that have been decorated by hand. Early printed books were laid out in the same way as manuscripts with wide margins and indentations in the text leaving blank spaces for decorated initial letters. It was sometimes intended that titles, chapter headings and capital letters be added by hand after printing. Many buyers wanted more than just these basic additions and decorated borders were sometimes added to pages, usually incorporating the owner's coat of arms. The page illustrated here is embellished with an initial letter in gold, borders in a pattern generally called 'white vine-stem', and a medallion portrait of Apuleius in the lower margin, probably copied from a Roman coin.

*[p.26]* Venus instructs Cupid to cause Psyche to fall in love with a monstrous creature.

[British Library C.105.g.6]

From *The Marriage of Cupid and Psyche, re-told by Walter Pater from 'The Golden Ass' of Lucius Apuleius*. Illustrated by Edmund Dulac. Limited Editions Club, New York, 1951.

Walter Pater's re-telling of the Cupid and Psyche story first published in his novel *Marius the Epicurean* in 1885, has several times been used as the text to accompany illustrated versions since. Pater, in introducing the story describes it as 'abounding in lovely visible imagery'. Edmund Dulac (1882–1953) was born in France, but resided in Britain for most of his life. His work was heavily influenced by eastern art. This was his last completed set of illustrations. It was the second book he was contracted to illustrate for the Limited Editions Club of New York; the first had been Pushkin's *The Golden Cockerel*. Dulac has set his illustrations in flattened circles intending to give the impression of looking into the bowl of a Greek cup. The book was published in an edition of 1,500 copies, all numbered and signed by Dulac.

*[p.28]* Psyche rescued by Zephyrus.

[British Library C.43.c.16]

From William Morris, *A Note by William Morris on his aims in founding the Kelmscott Press*. Kelmscott Press, 1898.

William Morris and the artist Sir Edward Burne-Jones collaborated in the 1860s on a proposed lavishly illustrated edition of Morris's long poetical work *The Earthly Paradise*, which included the tale of Cupid and Psyche. The project proved to be too ambitious for its time and had to be abandoned, but not before much work had been done, particularly on 'Cupid and Psyche'. At least 44 woodblocks were engraved for the story, many by Morris himself.

The volume illustrated was the last book from Morris' Kelmscott Press, and the frontispiece incorporating one of the 'Cupid and Psyche' engravings was the only one of the 'Earthly Paradise' illustrations to be published in the nineteenth century. An edition of 'Cupid and Psyche' printed from the surviving woodblocks was eventually published in 1974 by Clover Hill.

*[p.29]* Psyche discovers the identity of the sleeping Cupid.
[British Library C.99.b.32]
From Apuleius, *Cupid & Psyche. The most delectable tale of their marriage.* Engravings by Lettice Sandford. The Golden Cockerel Press, 1934.
This is one of the many finely printed private press editions of Apuleius' work to have appeared in this century. The Golden Cockerel Press was set up in 1920. It was taken over by the illustrator Robert Gibbings in 1924, before when little use had been made of illustration in its work. Gibbings ran the press until 1933, when it was taken over again by amongst others Christopher Sandford, who employed his wife Lettice to illustrate many of the books.
Lettice Sandford (b.1902) was primarily an engraver. She had studied under Graham Sutherland at Chelsea Polytechnic, and had also produced illustrations for the Boar's Head and Golden Hours Presses also run by her husband. She later illustrated volumes for the Folio Society.
*[p.31]* The tasks of Psyche.
[British Library 241.b.11]
From *La Psiche di Hercole Udine.* Venice, 1599.
This is probably the first edition of this work, a re-telling of Apuleius' story in epic verse. It is generally faithful to Apuleius' narrative, expanding on it in places. At the end he changes Cupid and Psyche's child from a girl to a boy named Diletto.
Each of the eight cantos is introduced by a detailed composite engraving which gives a pictorial summary of the incidents in that part of the story. The first of the engravings is signed 'I. valegio' (i.e. Giacomo Valegio), an artist and engraver working in Verona in the 16th century.

## THE LEGENDARY JOURNEYS OF ALEXANDER THE GREAT

*[p.34]* Olympias gives birth to Alexander the Great.
[British Library Royal MS 20 C.iii, f.15]
From *Historiae Alexandri Magni*, Bruges, 1490s.
In 1468 the Portuguese humanist Vasco da Lucena completed a French translation of one of the principal sources of our knowledge of the career of Alexander the Great. He dedicated his version of the *Historiae Alexandri Magni* by the first-century Roman author Quintus Curtius Rufus to Charles the Bold, Duke of Burgundy.
In addition to translating what remains of Curtius's text, Vasco attempted to fill in the losses that Curtius's History had suffered at an early date in its transmission. In particular he supplied a narrative to cover the events that elapsed between Alexander's birth in 356 BC and his entry into Phrygia in 333 BC which were originally covered in the lost first two books of the *Historiae.* As in the present case, most manuscripts mark the beginning of this section of of Vasco's text with a large miniature of the birth of Alexander. This episode was partly derived by the French author from the recent translation by Guarino of Verona of Plutarch's *Life of Alexander.*
*[p.36]* Scenes from the Romance of Alexander.
[British Library Royal MS 15 E.vi, f.18]
From the Old French Prose Alexander Romance. Rouen, 1445.
A popular thirteenth-century French prose version of the Alexander Romance is included in an extremely large manuscript containing a miscellany of medieval romances. This volume was produced in France for John Talbot, Earl of Shrewsbury, for presentation to Margaret of Anjou, probably in celebration of her marriage to Henry VI in 1445. The artist responsible for many of its 143 illustrations, 83 of which are dedicated to the story of Alexander, is known as the Talbot Master after his important contributions to this manuscript and two Books of Hours also made for the earl and countess. Another artist who worked on this volume painted his miniatures in the style of the Bedford Master, so named after his contribution to a sumptuous Book of Hours produced in Paris for the then regent of France, John, Duke of Bedford.
*[p.38]* Alexander rises into the heavens.
[British Library Royal MS 15 E.vi, f.20v]
From the Old French Prose Alexander Romance. Rouen, 1445, as p.36 above.
*[p.40]* Alexander's descent into the sea.
[British Library Royal MS 20 B.xx, f.77v]
From the Old French Prose Alexander Romance. Paris or Rouen, c.1425.

The same French prose version of Pseudo-Callisthenes that is contained in the Talbot miscellany is preserved in a heavily illustrated manuscript produced in France towards the end of the first quarter of the fifteenth century. Although much smaller in size and more obviously laid out as a picture book, this volume contains essentially the same cycle of illustrations. This fact reflects the common dependence of the illustrations of these two manuscripts and many others decorating texts in the romance tradition on a cycle which is thought to originate in late antiquity. The main artist responsible for the illustrations is named the Master of the Royal Alexander after this manuscript.

*[p.42 left]* Iskandar (Alexander) confers with the seven sages.

[British Library Or. MS 6810, f.214]

From Nizami, *Khamsa*. Timurid, later Herat style, 1494–95.

An important Persian descendant of the Greek Alexander Romance is contained in the *Khamsa* by the twelfth-century author Nizami (Abu Muhammad Ilyas ibn Yusuf ibn Mu'ayyad). Within this quintet of verse texts the story of Alexander is told in two parts, the *Sharafnama* (The Book of Honour) and *Iqbalnama* (The Book of Progress). The first of these narrates the main events of the Alexander legend and the second focuses on his prophethood and search for wisdom. Unlike Firdawsi Nizami accepts his Iskandar as the son of Philip of Macedon (Faylaqus). One particularly fine manuscript of the *Khamsa* was presented to Sultan Mirza Barlas, ruler of Samarkand. Among the miniatures that illustrate its Iqbalnama is a representation of Iskandar consulting the Seven Sages in which Iskandar is depicted in the likeness of Husayn Bayqara, the last Timurid ruler. This miniature and several others in the volume have been attributed to the painter Bihzad.

*[p.42 right]* Iskandar (Alexander) visits the sage.

[British Library Add. MS 27261, f.230]

From a Persian miscellany. Timurid, Shiraz, 1410–11.

Another manuscript that includes the *Sharafnama* is a miscellany copied by the scribes Muhammad al-Halva'i and Nasir al-katib for Iskandar Sultan (d. 1415). This volume is one of a small, but important group of manuscripts that were commissioned by Iskandar from Shiraz book-producers. Stylistically many of its illustrations anticipate the refinements achieved in later Timurid manuscripts.

*[p.43]* Alexander consults the Trees of the Sun and Moon.

[British Library Add. MS 15268, f.214]

From *Hisoire Universelle*. Acre, *c.*1285, as p.10.

## THE SEVEN VOYAGES OF SINDBAD THE SAILOR

*[p.44]* Sindbad the Sailor entertains Sindbad the Landsman.

[British Library K.T.C.102.b.2]

From *Sindbad the Sailor & other stories from the Arabian Nights*. Illustrated by Edmund Dulac. London, Hodder & Stoughton, [1914].

This is an example of the beautifully illustrated gift books produced by publishers at the beginning of the century for the Christmas market. They were generally also issued in de luxe limited editions, bound in vellum.

Edmund Dulac (1882–1953) was born in Toulouse but became a naturalised British subject. His delicate, detailed book illustrations were inspired by the art of the middle and far east. By the time he illustrated this selection of stories from *The Arabian Nights* his work was being heavily influenced by Persian miniatures. The pages all have patterned borders to give the effect of a Persian manuscript. Dulac was often drawn to the 'Nights' for subject matter. His first gift book for Hodder & Stoughton in 1907 had been a highly successful *Stories from the Arabian Nights*.

*[p.46]* A ship-wrecked sailor is rescued by a giant bird.

[British Library Or. MS 12220, f.72v]

From Al-Qazwini *Aja'ib al-Makhluqat* (Wonders of Creation). Timurid, Later Herat style, 1503–4.

Al-Qazwini (1203–83) was born in Persia, but lived most of his life in Baghdad (where the Sindbad stories are thought to have originated). Amongst the phenomena described in his *Wonders of Creation* are several stories probably originating from similar sources to those in 'Sindbad', including the tale illustrated here, which is reminiscent of Sindbad and the roc.

A man from the Persian city of Isfahan is so burdened with debts that he goes to sea with some merchants. They become trapped by a whirlpool and the man offers to sacrifice himself in the hope that the rest will be spared. He is abandoned on an island, and the ship is able to sail away. On the island is a huge tree where an enormous bird roosts. Finding the bird is not hostile, the man clings to one of its legs as it rises in the air and is carried across the sea to a village. After several days he walks to the seashore and encounters there the ship and companions with whom he had sailed.

*[p.49]* Sindbad stranded in the valley of diamonds.

[British Library 12410.ff.16]

From *Sindbad the Sailor and Ali Baba and the Forty Thieves*. London, Lawrence and Bullen, 1896. Illustrated by William Strang and J. B. Clark.

The illustration of Sindbad tied to a joint of meat is by William Strang R.A. (1859–1921). Strang was a painter and etcher born in Dumbarton. He studied at the Slade and between 1892 and 1902 concentrated on book illustration using both etchings and woodcuts. He and Joseph Benwell Clark had previously collaborated on an edition of *The Surprising Adventures of Baron Munchausen* in 1895.

*[p.50]* The canibal giant.

[British Library K.T.C.19.b.10]

From *The Arabian Nights Entertainments*. Selected and edited by Andrew Lang. Illustrated by Henry Justice Ford. London, Longmans, Green, and Co., 1898.

Henry Justice Ford (1860–1941), worked as a painter, exhibiting regularly at the Royal Academy, but is best known as an illustrator – particularly for his collaborations with Andrew Lang and his wife Leonora. Andrew Lang (1844–1912) was a writer, Greek scholar and anthropologist, much interested in folk-lore and the origins of myth. He edited the 12 coloured Fairy Books (The Blue Fairy Book of 1889 through to the Lilac Fairy Book of 1910), most of which were illustrated by Ford.

Ford's black and white illustrations use delicate and decorative pen-work, but as in this illustration, he produced very strong and powerful images. The framework of the picture barely contains the threatening one-eyed giant and the terrified sailors are forced into the corner of the picture space.

*[p.51]* Sindbad rests and refreshes himself.

[British Library 12410.ff.16]

From *Sindbad the Sailor and Ali Baba and the Forty Thieves*. London, Lawrence and Bullen, 1896. Illustrated by William Strang and J. B. Clark, as *p.49* above.

*[p.52]* The Old Man of the Sea.

[British Library Or. MS 4383, f.49r]

From Al-Qazwini, *Aja'ib al-Makhluqat (Wonders of Creation)*. Qajar, 1834.

Al-Qazwini's *Wonders of Creation* was so popular, that lavishly illustrated manuscripts were still being produced in Persia and India in the nineteenth century.

The story illustrated here is similar to that of the Old Man of the Sea in 'Sindbad'. A man abandoned on an island, rests under some fruit trees, where are seated some handsome men with no bones in their legs. One of them suddenly jumps upon his neck and winds his legs around his throat, urging him to get up and carry him around the island while he picks fruit from the trees for himself and his companions. He is unable to remove him until he is blinded by a thorn in his eye, whereupon the man intoxicates him with pressed grapes and is able to loosen his grip and free himself.

*[p.53]* Sindbad takes his master to the elephant graveyard.

[British Library 12410.t.2]

From *The Arabian Nights. Tales from the Thousand and One Nights*. Illustrated by E. J. Detmold. London, Hodder and Stoughton, [1924].

Edward Julius Detmold (1883–1957) was an etcher and watercolour painter who produced illustrations for a number of books between 1899 and 1924, mainly of natural history subjects. His early work was in collaboration with his twin brother Charles Maurice, who comitted suicide in 1908. Their style was heavily influenced by Japanese art. Edward continued to produce work after his brother's death. *The Arabian Nights* which he illustrated in 1924 proved to be ideal subject matter. He was able to combine natural detail with the style and delicacy of Persian miniatures to produce exquisite and fantastic images.

## RAMA'S QUEST FOR SITA

*[p.55]* Rama, Sita and Lakshmana begin their life of exile in the forest.

[British Library Add. MS 15296(1), f.70r]

By Sahib Din, Udaipur, 1650. From the third or Forest-book of the Ramayana.

This illustration is from the great manuscript of Valmiki's *Ramayana* prepared for Rana Jagat Singh of Mewar from 1649 to 1653 in the court studio at Udaipur in southern Rajasthan. The manuscript is on the largest scale, each of the seven books being illustrated by up to 100 paintings, with the paintings occupying the whole page. The different books are in three different but contemporary styles of Mewar painting, including one heavily influenced by painting from the Deccan.

Manuscripts of the Ramayana with illustrations are not known before the 16th century. The earliest surviving such manuscript is, paradoxically, the manuscript of the Persian translation from the Sanskrit prepared for the Mughal emperor Akbar in 1588, now in Jaipur, whose wonderful miniatures make it one of the greatest of Indian manuscripts. Other Ramayana manuscripts were illustrated in many of the Rajput courts, as well as at the Rajput courts in the Punjab Hills. Rama was of the Ikshvaku race, descended from the Sun, and Rajput clans of the Solar dynasty, among them the rulers of Mewar, claimed Rama as their ancestor. The Ramayana thus became part of family history, and illustrated manuscripts of it were produced rather like the ancestral histories of the Mughals.

*[p.56]* Rama and Lakshmana guided by a sage set out to win Sita.
[British Library Add. Or. 3829]
Painted by the Maithil Brahmini Sita Devi, Jitwarpur village, Madhubani, Bihar, July 1974.
Women in the villages of north Bihar traditionally paint auspicious scenes on the walls of the bridal chambers of their houses, where newly married couples spend their first night together. Few images could be more auspicious for a marriage than one invoking the marriage of Rama and Sita. Sita's position here reflects her imaginary presence, since realistic spatial conventions play no part in this type of painting. Designs for a family's marriage paintings would traditionally be carried in women's heads, since as girls they would help the elder women prepare the rooms. Sometimes the designs would be committed to paper as aides-mémoire, as here.

*[p.59]* Sita has been captured by Ravana, who keeps her prisoner in the beautiful grove of ashoka trees in his palace in Lanka.
[British Library IO 3621, f.3r]
Udaipur, *c.*1650. From the fifth or Beautiful-book of the Ramayana, as *p.55* above.

*[p.61]* Rama and his monkey and bear allies begin the attack on Lanka.
[British Library Add. MS 15297(1), f.29r]
By Sahib Din, Udaipur, 1653. From the sixth or Battle-book of the Ramayana, as *p.55* above.

*[p.62]* Hanuman in single combat with Ravana.
[British Library Add. Or. 891]
By a Kalighat artist, Calcutta, *c.*1865.
Popular devotion to the monkey Hanuman elevated him to the chiefest of all Rama's allies. Here he is engaged in mortal combat with the demon-king Ravana himself. Kalighat in south Calcutta is the site of one of the most important Hindu temples in Bengal, dedicated to the fearsome goddess Kali. It was famous in the 19th century for its popular devotional paintings, turned out by the local artists for pilgrims to the temple, both as souvenirs of the visit and as icons for worship.

## JOURNEY TO THE WEST

*[p.64]* The Sage Mother of Dongling rises on a cloud accompanied by a phoenix-like green bird, before a crowd of admirers.
[British Library Add. MS 22689]
From *Yuntai xianrui* [Keepsake from the Cloud Gallery]. Text and illustrations on paper in a large concertina album. Ink, gold and colours on paper. 1750.
In the novel *Xiyouji* [Journey to the West], Wu Cheng'en, the author, weaves spiritual and temporal aspects of traditional Chinese society into an ingenious narrative concerned with the search for the truth as embodied in Buddhist texts and ultimate salvation. The Daoist search for immortality, for example, is frequently touched on, as are Daoist accomplishments, such as alchemy and travelling through the skies on clouds. One of Monkey's most useful supernatural skills is his ability to traverse great distances by means of a cloud trapeze. The painting reproduced here, the first of 16 which are concerned with Daoist adepts and immortality depicts the Sage Mother of Dongling. Having applied herself to the Dao (Tao, 'Way') was greatly skilled in the arts of medicinal healing. One day before a throng of admirers she rose on a cloud accompanied by a green phoenix-like bird. Many Chinese had long been obsessed with longevity and immortality. It is executed in a meticulous version of the 'green and gold', or 'blue and green' style of painting, an archaistic style which was used to recall the past. This style was used during the Tang (618–906 AD), the period in which the real journey to India took place and in which the novel is set. From the colophon inscribed on the front of the album case and the subject matter it appears that it was commissioned for a person of considerable age.

*[p.68]* Xuanzang receiving the sutras from Buddha in Paradise.
[British Library Or. 64.b.16]
Frontispiece illustration to the 'Perfection of Wisdom'. *Mahāprajñāpāramitāsūtra* (Jap.: *Dai hannya haramitta-kyō*. Kofukuji Temple, Nara, Japan; 1383 or earlier. Folding volume. Ink and mixture of gampi and mulberry paper. 29 × 9.6 cm.
In the same way as the written canons of Buddhism had to be transmitted to China from India, so too did they have to be conveyed to other Southeast and East Asian countries. In this Japanese hand copied text, the Chinese pilgrim Xuanzang is depicted as receiving the Buddhist holy scriptures (sutras) from the Buddha who is seated on a lotus throne and surrounded by clouds and deities. The sutras are shown as scrolls stacked inside the bamboo frame that Xuanzang carries on his back. In reality Xuanzang travelled through the kingdoms of Chinese Central Asia to modern India to search for Buddhist texts. However, in recognition of the importance of this quest India, in the novel, becomes synonymous with the Buddhist Paradise.
*[p.70]* Pigsy succumbs to earthly desires by accepting food, observed by Monkey and Xuanzang.
[British Library 15271.c.13]
Illustration from *Xiyouji* [Journey to the West] by Wu Cheng'en. Woodblock edition; 18th century.
Adherence to Buddhist precepts, such as resisting earthly desires, is addressed in the novel. Here Pigsy accepts food while Monkey looks on and Xuanzang, their master, sits aloof. That much of what is regarded as reality is mere illusion is demonstrated in this episode when it becomes apparent that the food has no substance. Such incidents recall other tests set for the pilgrims in their quest for the Buddhist holy scriptures (sutras) in which they are confronted by supernatural phenomena and monsters.
*[p.72]* Monkey with his iron staff and Pigsy with his muck rake engage the Bull Demon King.
[British Library 15271.c.13]
Illustration from *Xiyouji* [Journey to the West] by Wu Cheng'en. Woodblock edition; 18th century.
The physical trials of everyday life are alluded to as the five pilgrims are confronted with 80 obstacles to overcome on their journey to India, or Paradise. Here, Monkey and Pigsy take on the Bull Demon King. Having obtained the sutras the return journey proves no less perilous when the bodhisattva Guanyin orders one more catastrophe. All, including some of the scriptures, are soaked or lost, as they were on the real return to China, as they attempt to cross the River that Flows to Heaven on the back of the White Turtle. This brings the total number of calamities to 81. As this is the perfect number in Chinese cosmological numerology, it adds yet another miraculous element to the tale.


THE LIFE OF ST BRENDAN

*[p.74]* Deluded sailors prepare a meal on a whale that they have mistaken for an island.
[British Library Harley MS 4751, f.69]
From a Latin bestiary, c.1230–1240
Bestiary lore believed whales stayed on the surface long enough for plants to grow in the sand. Small fish were drawn into the whale's mouth by the sweet smell that it emitted. Generally in the bestiary, but not in Brendan's case, the heat of the fire caused the whale to dive, dragging the sailors with it. Christian allegory saw these unfortunates as those who trusted in the devil.
This Latin bestiary is illustrated with 106 dramatic miniatures. The often fanciful accounts of animal behaviour in the bestiaries generally permitted allegorical interpretations. Thus, the fish attracted by the whale's scent are identified as those who succumb to the lure of sinful temptations.
*[p.76]* Brendan and his crew disembark on what they take to be an island but is in reality the back of a benevolent whale.
[British Library G. 7237]
A map showing St Brendan's isle, in *Nova typis transacta navigatio Novi Orbis Indiae Occidentalis . . .*, 1621, compiled by Honorius Philoponus [i.e. Gaspar Plautius]
Brendan's goal, the Land of Promise of the Saints is located to the north in this map. In other maps its location is more southerly. This account of the mission of the Benedictine monks under the Catalan Bernat Boïl, who accompanied Columbus on his second crossing to the New World includes an account of Brendan's voyage. The work was compiled by one 'Honorius Philoponus', generally taken to be Gaspar Plautius, Abbot of the Austrian monastery of Seitenstetten. The map offers a more plausible location for St Brendan's isle than many earlier ones.

## THE QUEST FOR THE HOLY GRAIL

*[p.82]* Miniature from the opening leaf of the *Estoire del Saint Graal*.
[British Library Royal MS 14.E.iii, f.3 (detail)]
From *Estoire del Saint Graal* [History of the Holy Grail], Northern France, early fourteenth century.
This manuscript contains three of the six prose romances that make up the so-called Vulgate Cycle: the *Estoire*, the *Queste del Saint Graal*, and the *Mort Artu* [Death of King Arthur]. A particularly fine manuscript, it is generously illustrated with one hundred and five miniatures. The frontispieces to each of the three parts also display excellent architectural details and numerous examples of drolleries: amusing or grotesque figures of humans or animals, or combining features of both, which are frequent in the margins of medieval manuscripts. The *Estoire* tells the early history of the Grail before its appearance to the knights of King Arthur.

*[p.84 left]* Miniature from the opening leaf of the *Estoire del Saint Graal*.
[British Library Royal MS 14.E.iii, f.3 (detail)]
From *Estoire del Saint Graal* [History of the Holy Grail], Northern France, early fourteenth century, as *p.80* above.

*[p.84 right]* Josephe, Bishop of Sarras, promises to entrust the Holy Grail when he dies to Alain, the twelfth son of Bron.
[British Library Add. MS 10292, f.65]
From *Estoire del Saint Graal* (History of the Holy Grail), Northern France, early fourteenth century.
British Library Additional Manuscripts 10292–94 comprise all six parts of the Vulgate cycle: the *Estoire*, *Merlin* and its continuation, *Lancelot*, the *Queste*, and the *Mort Artu*. Like Royal MS 14.E.iii, it is illustrated with nearly 750 miniatures, many of which have a similar model as the Royal manuscript. The *Estoire* tells how Joseph of Arimathea brought the Grail to Britain.

*[p.85 left]* Seven flaming hands appear and cast fire upon Moys.
[British Library Royal MS 14.E.iii, f.76v]
From *Estoire del Saint Graal* [History of the Holy Grail], Northern France, early fourteenth century, as *p.82* above.

*[p.85 right]* A wounded knight, carried on a litter, awaits the appearance of the Grail.
[British Library Royal MS 14.E.iii, f.99]
From *Estoire del Saint Graal* [History of the Holy Grail], Northern France, early fourteenth century, as *p.82* above.
The *Queste* follows in detail the efforts of several of Arthur's knights to achieve the quest. Lancelot fails because of his previous adultery with Guinevere.

*[p.86]* Galahad arrives at an abbey.
[British Library Royal MS 14.E.iii, f.93v]
From *Estoire del Saint Graal* [History of the Holy Grail], Northern France, early fourteenth century, as *p.82* above.
This miniature occurs in the second part of Royal MS 14.E.iii, the *Queste del Saint Graal*, which tells of the departure of the knights of Arthur's court in search of the Grail and culminates in Galahad's successful completion of the quest and the Grail's appearance at Sarras.

*[p.89]* Galahad, sitting in the Siege Perilous.
[Paris, Bibliothèque Nationale MS Fr. 120, f.524v]
From the *Queste del Saint Graal*, France, early fifteenth century.
This manuscript forms part of a complete Vulgate Cycle (MSS Fr. 117–20). It is finely illuminated and was acquired in 1405 by Jean, Duc de Berry, a connoisseur and owner of many splendid manuscripts. When it passed into the possession of Jean's great-grandson, Jacques d'Armagnac, Duke of Nemours, the latter had many of the miniatures, including this one, repainted in keeping with the taste of the mid-fifteenth century.

# Further reading

GENERAL

Joseph Campbell, *The Hero with a Thousand Faces* (Princeton, 1949; reprinted London: Fontana, 1993)
G. S. Kirk, *Myth: its Meaning and Functions in Ancient and Other Cultures* (Cambridge, 1971)
G. S. Kirk, *The Nature of Greek Myths* (Harmondsworth, 1974)
K. K. Ruthven, *Myth* (London, 1976)
Jane Davidson Reid, *The Oxford Guide to Classical Mythology in the Arts, 1300–1990s* (New York and Oxford, 1993)
Otto Rank, Lord Raglan, Alan Dundes, *In Quest of the Hero* (Princeton, 1990)
Arthur Cotterell, *A Dictionary of World Mythology* (Oxford, 1986)


THE EPIC OF GILGAMESH

*The Epic of Gilgamesh*, translated with an introduction by N. K. Sanders, Penguin Classics (Harmondsworth, 1960; reprinted with revisions 1964)
Henrietta McCall, *Mesopotamian Myths. The Legendary Past* (London, 1990)
*Myths from Mesopotamia: Creation, The Flood, Gilgamesh and Others*, translated with an introduction and notes by Stephanie Dalley (Oxford, 1989)


JASON AND THE QUEST FOR THE GOLDEN FLEECE

Robert Graves, *The Golden Fleece* (London, 1944)
Apollonius Rhodius, *The Voyage of the Argo. The Argonautica*, translated by E. V. Rieu (Harmondsworth, 1959)
Apollonius of Rhodes, *Jason and the Golden Fleece (The Argonautica)* translated by Richard Hunter (Oxford, 1993; reprinted 1995)
Apollonius of Rhodes, *Argonautica Book III*, edited by R. L. Hunter (Cambridge, 1989; reprinted 1995)


THE HOMECOMING OF ODYSSEUS

Homer, *The Odyssey*, translated by Richmond Lattimore (New York, 1965)
Piero Boitani, *The Shadows of Ulysses. Figures of a Myth* (Oxford, 1994)
W. B. Stanford, *The Ulysses Theme. A Study in the Adaptability of a Traditional Hero* (Oxford, 1954; 2nd edition 1963)
Jasper Griffin, *The Odyssey* (Cambridge, 1987)
W. B. Stanford and J. V. Luce, *The Quest for Ulysses* (London, 1974)
Beaty Rubens and Oliver Taplin, *An Odyssey round Odysseus. The Man and his Story traced through time and place* (London, 1989)


THE TALE OF CUPID AND PSYCHE

Apuleius, *The Golden Ass*, translated by Robert Graves (London, 1990)
Apuleius, *The story of Cupid and Psyche as related by Apuleius*, edited with introduction and notes by Louis C. Purser (London, 1910)
Elizabeth Hazelton Haight, *Apuleius and his Influence* (London, 1927)
Carl C. Schlam, *The Metamorphoses of Apuleius* (London, 1992)

James Tatum, *Apuleius and The Golden Ass* (Ithaca and London, 1979)
P. G. Walsh, *The Roman Novel* (Cambridge, 1970)


THE LEGENDARY JOURNEYS OF ALEXANDER THE GREAT

George Cary, *The Medieval Alexander*, edited by D. J. A. Ross (Cambridge, 1956; reprinted New York, 1987)
D. J. A. Ross, *Alexander Historiatus. A Guide to Medieval Illustrated Alexander Literature* (London, 1963; 2nd edition Frankfurt am Main, 1988)
*Iskandarnamah. A Persian Medieval Alexander-Romance*, translated by Minoo S. Southgate (New York, 1978)
*The Greek Alexander Romance*, translated by Richard Stoneman (Harmondsworth, 1991)
*Legends of Alexander the Great*, edited by Richard Stoneman (London and Richmond, Vermont, 1994)
*Alessandro Magno: Storia e Mito*, catalogue of the exhibition held at the Palazzo Ruspoli, Rome, edited by Antonio Di Vita (Italian-language, Rome, 1995)


THE SEVEN VOYAGES OF SINDBAD THE SAILOR

*The Thousand and One Nights*, translated by Edward William Lane (London, 1839–41)
*A Plain and Literal Translation of the Arabian Nights' Entertainments*, translated by Richard F. Burton (Kamashastra Society, Benares [i.e. Stoke Newington], 1885–88)
*Tales from the Thousand and One Nights*, translated by N. J. Dawood (Penguin, London, 1973)
*The Arabian Nights in English Literature*, edited by Peter L. Caracciolo (London, 1988)
Mia I. Gerhardt, *The Art of Storytelling: a Literary Study of the Thousand and One Nights* (Leiden, 1963)
Robert Irwin, *The Arabian Nights: a Companion* (London, 1994)


RAMA'S QUEST FOR SITA

*The Ramayana of Valmiki*, translated by Hari Prasad Shastri (London, 3 vols., 1952–59)
*The Ramayana of Valmiki*, translation edited by Robert P. Goldman (Princeton, 1984–   [In progress])
*Ramayana* [retold by] William Buck (Berkeley/London, 1976)
J. L. Brockington, *Righteous Rama, the Evolution of an Epic* (Oxford/Delhi, 1985)
*The Holy Lake of the Acts of Rama*, translated by W. Douglas (2nd impression, Delhi, 1971)
*Many Ramayanas: The Diversity of a Narrative Tradition in South Asia*, edited by Paula Richman (Berkeley, 1991)
H. D. Sankalia, *The Ramayana in Historical Perspective* (New Delhi, 1982)
P. Banerjee, *Rama in Indian Literature, Art and Thought* (New Delhi, 1986)
Romila Thapur, *Exile and the Kingdom, Some Thoughts on the Ramayana* (Bangalore, 1978)
*The Story of Prince Rama* [told by] Brian Thompson [with manuscript paintings] (Harmondsworth, 1980)
*The Adventure of Rama* [retold by] M. C. Beach, with illustrations from a Sixteenth-century Mughal Manuscript (Washington DC, 1983)
N. Poovaya-Smith, J. P. Losty, and Jane Bevan, *Manuscript Paintings from the Ramayana* (Bradford, 1989)
*The Legend of Rama: Artistic Visions*, edited by Vidya Dehejia (Bombay, 1994)


JOURNEY TO THE WEST

Wu Ch'eng-en, *Monkey*, Arthur Waley trans. (London,  1984) [First edition 1942] [partial translation]
Wu Cheng'en, *Journey to the West*, W. J. F. Jenner trans. (Beijing, 1982) (3 vols)
*Dear Monkey*, translated from the Chinese by Arthur Waley, abridged by Alison Waley (Glasgow and London, 1973)
*The Legend of the Monkey King* [translation of *Xiyouji gushi* by Wu Cheng'en and Ruo Gu; English version by George Theiner], (London, 1992)

*Further Reading*

Glen Dudbridge, 'The Hundred-chapter Hsi-yu chi and its Early Versions', *Asia Major*, New Series, 14 (1969), pp. 141–216
Anthony C. Yu 'Hsi-yu chi', in William H. Nienhauser ed., *The Indiana Companion to Traditional Chinese Literature*, pp. 413–418 (Bloomington, 1986) [extensive bibliography]
Sally Hovey Wriggins, *Xuanzang: a Buddhist Pilgrim on the Silk Road* (Boulder, 1996)


THE LIFE OF ST BRENDAN

*Navigatio Sancti Brendani Abbatis from Early Latin Manuscripts*, edited with introduction and notes by Carl Selmer (Notre Dame, Indiana, 1959; reprinted Dublin, 1989)
Tim Severin, *The Brendan Voyage* (London, 1978; reprinted 1996)
*The Voyage of St Brendan, in Lives of the Saints*, translated with an introduction by J. F. Webb, Penguin Classics (Harmondsworth, 1965)


THE QUEST FOR THE HOLY GRAIL

Several of the major Grail romances are available in English translation in the Penguin Classics series: *Peredur, in The Mabinogion*; Chrétien de Troyes's *Conte del Graal*, in his *Arthurian Romances*; *The Quest of the Holy Grail* (translation of the *Queste del Saint Graal*); *The Death of King Arthur* (translation of the *Mort Artu*); Wolfram von Eschenbach, *Parzifal*. Malory's *Le Morte d'Arthur* is available in the same series.
Elizabeth Jenkins, *The Mystery of King Arthur* (London, 1975)
Roger Sherman Loomis, *The Grail: from Celtic Myth to Christian Symbol* (New York, 1963; reprinted London, 1992)
D. D. R. Owen, *The Evolution of the Grail Legend*, St Andrews University Publications, 58 (Edinburgh & London, 1968)
Jessie Weston, *From Ritual to Romance* (Cambridge, 1920; reprinted Princeton, N.J., 1993)
Muriel Whitaker, *The Legends of King Arthur in Art*, Arthurian Studies, 22 (Cambridge, 1990)